THE ART OF BEGINNING

This publication was financially supported by the Agricultural University, Wageningen, the Netherlands

THE ART OF

First experiences and problems of Western expatriates in
developing countries with special emphasis on
rural development and rural education

BEGINNING

Editor: Wout van den Bor

 Pudoc Wageningen 1983

Illustrations: Debora Goedewaagen, Groningen

CIP-GEGEVENS

Art

The art of beginning : first experiences and problems of
western expatriates in developing countries with special
emphasis on rural development and rural education /
ed. Wout van den Bor ; [ill. Debora Goedewaagen]. –
Wageningen : Pudoc. – Ill.
Met lit. opg.
ISBN 90-220-0817-7
SISO 354.7 UDC 339.9
Trefw. : ontwikkelingshulp / rurale ontwikkeling.

ISBN 90-220-0817-7

© Centre for Agricultural Publishing and Documentation (Pudoc), Wageningen, 1983

Printed in the Netherlands

CONTENTS

V

ACKNOWLEDGEMENTS

Some books are the result of the efforts of one single person. Other books can be published because many people have co-operated in realizing a common goal. This book is an example of the latter. It would hardly be possible to mention everyone who took part in the preparatory phase and who has been of assistance during the compilation of this book. Nevertheless, I do thank them all from the bottom of my heart. Without their spiritual, intellectual and material support, here in Europe as well as in Africa, the final result would have been no more than an interesting idea.

There remain a number of people to whom I feel compelled to express my special gratitude. First, I am greatly indebted to Professor Jaap van Bergeijk, who, once he is convinced of the usefulness of an initiative, supports it with energy and perseverance. His interest and fruitful advice during the various phases of this project have contributed more than he may surmise. I also thank my colleagues of the Department of Education and Teacher Training of the Agricultural University for their mental support, in particular Theo M. P. Oltheten. When I was preparing my field trip I made grateful use of the practical advice of Wim Nijwening, who was at the time teaching at the School for Higher Agricultural Education in Dronten.

When I made my journey through Africa I was entirely dependent on the good-will and help of my hosts and hostesses. I thank them sincerely for their co-operation and hospitality, especially Father R. Tielen in Kenya and Frère Mébius Hettinga in Yaounde. I have learned much from the personal experiences of Arie Wingelaar, who has lived and worked in different parts of Africa and Latin America, and who now teaches at Barneveld College in The Netherlands. I am grateful for the assistance offered to me by the staff and field workers of the Organization of Netherlands Volunteers in The Hague, Tanzania, Zambia, Botswana, Cameroon and Ivory Coast. Jan and Lies Siemonsma, who were at that time in charge of the Centre Néerlandais in Abidjan did everything possible to make my stay in Ivory Coast useful and pleasant. I wish to gratefully acknowledge the help given to me by the staff of the Dutch Embassies in Nairobi, Dar es Salaam, Lusaka, Gaborone, Yaounde and Abidjan. Nor can I forget the organizational assistance and personal involvement of Hans Kats, Dutch Agricultural Attaché in Abidjan.

Many people have offered me accommodation and transportation; without their spontaneous generosity my journey would not have been so successful.

1

I thank all the co-authors of this book for giving me some of their time and for their valuable contributions, which have made this book a real joint venture.

While compiling this publication I received highly-valued editorial assistance from the publishers, particularly from Ian Cressie and Rob Aalpol.

Cis Doorman, Annemarie van Droffelaar-Morsch and Jannet Hadders typed the different versions of the manuscript without any complaint and Monique Calon translated substantial parts of the book into English. I am greatly indebted to them all.

Last but not least, I express my gratitude to the Board of the Agricultural University of Wageningen for their financial support and for the trust they have put in me.

Wout van den Bor

2

PREFACE

Some years ago, I was taking a walk with Wout van den Bor, initiator, editor and co-author of this book. We talked about the problems of young teachers of agriculture, who, having grown up and received their education in the industrialized society of their fatherland, are faced with the difficult task of developing agricultural knowledge, skills and attitudes among people of all ages in the Third World. We both agreed that these teachers could learn much from each other, if given the opportunity to exchange experiences. Awareness of and reacting to educational problems experienced by others has since time immemorial proven to be a valuable method of mastering unruly situations. How could this method be employed to benefit the work of young teachers of agriculture in developing countries, to help this large group of development workers whose idealism and expertise do not alter the fact that they remain 'strangers and spectators' amidst the obliging natives of the country? An interesting question. One which cannot be answered by discussing it in the course of a short walk.

It is now 1983 and much has happened that may contribute towards answering this question. Wout van den Bor has in the meantime not remained idle. Once a problem has been brought to his attention it is not long before he steps into your office with a number of ideas about how to solve it; not merely suggestions but carefully considered plans, in which competence, insight and idealism are accompanied by a considerable dose of reality. This book is the evidence that, in this case too, the plan did not fail to materialize.

'The Art of Beginning' does not belong to the category of books that find their origins solely in the author's urge to write from his comfortable niche between desk and bookcase. It came to be through discussions and agreement with pioneering teachers of agriculture who are employed as development workers in widely dispersed areas of the African continent. To encourage them to reflect upon, write about and gain more insight into their experiences as teachers, Wout van den Bor embarked, in the summer of 1980, on an extensive journey throughout a number of African countries. He visited the contributors to this book on location – the places about which they have written – and exchanged ideas with them about the goals of their co-operative effort to write a story. I have a reason for using the word story. The reason being that Hans Visser (Kenya), Gerrit Noordam (Kenya), Gerrit J. Koeslag (Tanzania), David and Hennie van der Schans (Tanzania), Jan Willem Bulthuis (Zambia), Ben Veldboom (Zambia), Willem Zijp (Lesotho), Piet van der Poel (Botswana), Theo Groot

(Zaire), Nicolien Wassenaar (Cameroon), and Goof Bus (Ivory Coast) have, under the editorial guidance of Wout van den Bor, certainly not written a dull treatise about bottlenecks or good and bad luck as seen and recorded from an objective distance. They have instead told a human story, a story of people who show that they are involved not only with their heads but also with their hearts. The source of their contributions is the real life situation, a reality in which they must act and in which the faculties of the mind and those of the heart are closely knit. If one aims at getting to the heart of these matters, one will gladly use the metaphor, as words do not suffice.

I think that this is a special book. Special because of its contents, the way in which the contents are presented, the way in which the various contributions have been arranged to form a harmonious composition, the way in which they have been placed in an educational framework – and also special because of its goal: to inform and encourage all who are working in rural development in Third World countries. Gaining knowledge from each other's experiences can lead to a different perspective on one's own problems and contribute to learning how to solve these problems. However, a certain amount of imagination is and remains an indispensible asset for every pioneer. That a more exquisite parable exists than that with which Wout van den Bor concludes this book is beyond my imagination. I sincerely hope that this book will find its way into the hands of interested readers, both here in the Netherlands and abroad.

Jaap van Bergeijk
Professor of Education
Agricultural University
Wageningen, the Netherlands

4

1 HOW AN UNUSUAL BOOK CAME TO BE

Wout van den Bor

A USEFUL CONVERSATION

'To be quite honest with you', said the publisher, who had cordially invited me to discuss my ideas about this book with him, 'I am somewhat perplexed. It's the first time I've been faced with a book like this. Please understand, I like the stories very much, but on reading parts of the book some questions come to mind.'

He glanced at me and hesitated . . .

'Well, can you tell me a little more about the purpose of the book?'

'With pleasure', I said. 'This book presents authentic accounts of first experiences and problems of Western expatriates working in developing countries. The essays in the book refer to activities in rural development, with special emphasis on rural education. I hope the book will be used by people who are preparing for an assignment abroad, as well as by anyone who is interested in the difficult position of expatriates working in a developing country. The aim of the book is to encourage development workers to prepare thoroughly for their assignments. To do this they have to be told in detail what they can expect when they start their work in a developing country.'

The publisher clearly wasn't quite satisfied with my answer. He leafed through the pages of the drafts I'd sent and said, 'The stories are rather interesting and very instructive, but I'm not so sure of their scientific value. And why are they written and edited in this rather unconventional way?'

'Agreed', I said. 'I admit it is not scientific in the usual sense of the word, nor is it Hemingway, but what can you expect from a group of people, chosen more or less at random, who have written about their most vital experiences, their everyday problems. They're not professional writers or scientists, but what is more important, scientific and literary merit or genuineness and practical worth?'

The publisher nodded and said, 'I really want to be of help to you but you will have to give me some time to think about this. I'll let you know my decision'.

I said I understood and left the publisher to ruminate over my manuscript. On my way home I couldn't help thinking that the publisher had touched on a shortcoming when he had asked me to clarify the aim of the book. He hadn't quite understood, and he had been able to talk to me. What of my readers – they would have to be told more. It was going to be an unusual book all right.

This book can be seen as having three parts. In the first part I try to explain more fully the reasons why I have compiled the book. The second, and major, part comprises eleven essays from development workers in the field, describing the problems they faced when starting their assignments. In the third part (the second last chapter), I indicate some of the main trends in the essays and draw some conclusions that I hope will contribute in the future towards the training of development workers, especially in agricultural education. Although it is chiefly a book about problems, it is not all gloom and doom; there are suggestions and solutions offered. My aim throughout is to encourage development workers to prepare thoroughly for their assignments abroad.

SOME IMPORTANT QUESTIONS

On many occasions it has struck me that so many expatriates, on returning to their own country, have to admit that they were often at a loss as to what to do during their first months in the field. How can I explain the fact that it takes them such a long time to get down to the work for which they came? Why is it all so difficult at first? Should they have had more answers to questions, or more to the point, should they have asked themselves more questions before boarding the plane for their assignment abroad.

Let me formulate some of these, perhaps even frightening, questions. 'Why did I chose development work?' In most cases the answer can be easily found. Our worldly goods are very unjustly divided. Hunger, poverty and disease exist and something must be done about this. Bridges and hospitals must be built. Teachers are needed for schools and food production must be increased enormously. This is easy to understand. But if our man probes deeper, he'd soon find himself asking another question. 'Why do I actually want to work in a developing country?' Why indeed. Could he not just as well work here, in the Netherlands, or somewhere nearby? That might be even better. After all, people must be made aware of the gigantic problems in developing countries. This awareness must eventually lead them to give more money or to take political action.

Some people might say: 'What a lot of unnecessary soul-searching. As long as you do your job well and what is expected of you, it really doesn't matter whether you are an adventurer seeking the rays of the tropical sun or an idealist who flew the nest to relieve others of their daily trials and poverty.' I, for one, do not share this opinion. I think that personal motives that have not been well-considered, and are therefore often unrealistic, may be one of the reasons that a development worker is unable to function properly in his job, and that causes him eventually to mourn: 'I don't understand why things haven't worked out the way they should have, I really tried'. This situation relates directly to the purpose of this book.

Are there other important questions to consider? Certainly. For example, how should the beginning development worker behave in that faraway country? What should his approach be? What is the best course, to take the plunge right away or observe from the sidelines for a while? Should he try to become good friends with the local people as soon as possible or keep his distance at first? Should he come to agreements with this counterpart immediately or first let himself be guided by his counterpart? A number of things will have been decided beforehand; much however will have to be dealt with once he has arrived at his destination.

Clearly, all the questions I have posed are leading to one single question with two important components: 'Is it worthwhile to prepare yourself for your future work situation in a developing country, and is it possible?' Some people don't bother to distinguish these two components and reach a very unsatisfactory conclusion. They argue that the situation in each developing country is so completely different and that it is therefore practically impossible to prepare yourself.' Make sure that you have mastered your trade or profession,' they say, 'learn the basics of the language and see what happens. Everyone needs time to adapt. That's inevitable. Learning by trial and error is preferable to wasting time and money on preparations that will probably prove to have been of no avail.' The reader will understand that I do not belong to the category of people who hold this opinion. If that had been the case I would never have compiled this book. In my opinion people who are planning to do development work should do their utmost to be well prepared for their future task. I will try to illustrate this point by means of an example.

A SAD STORY

Somewhere in the vast blue Caribbean Sea there is a small island. Fifteen hundred people, descendants of black African slaves, live on the island. A north-east trade wind blows constantly across the dry acacia bushes. It's an arid country. From the air, traces of long neglected plantations can be seen. Now, only small-scale agriculture and horticulture are practised. It's a pity, because the island is isolated and the food supply must be flown in on a small plane. As a result, food is expensive, yet there are very few ways of earning a living on the island.

The island is fertile, but for some reason the people have turned their back to the land. It's a sad situation, but true. The government of the country to which the island belongs asks the former European colonizer to send a horticulturist, for the people must return to the land. The man is found. Let's call him Peter[1]. He has just completed his education in horticulture. When asked if he is interested in going to the island he accepts enthusiastically. He has never worked in a developing country. He is informed about the condition of the soil and the climate and realizes that he will have to organize some means of irrigation there. On arrival, Peter starts by setting up an experimental garden. There is more than enough land. He also has

---

1   The island exists, so does the horticulturist. However, this example has nothing to do with his specific project.

plans of giving an elementary course on growing vegetables. Everything goes slowly at first, but Peter isn't worried, after all he has three years the time.

At the end of the first year, he starts worrying. The vegetables in the experimental garden are growing well, but no one comes to his demonstration days. The co-operative he established isn't doing very well either. The people in charge are continually arguing and forget that there's more important work to be done. Gradually the number of people attending his course dwindle. After two years on the island Peter is really worried. It's futile to continue giving the course because it doesn't seem to have produced any results whatsoever. He's at odds with the local shopkeepers because he sells his vegetables for a much lower price than they do. The local government has turned its back on him too – somehow he hasn't lived up to their expectations.

Peter writes to his employer in Europe, to ask for an assistant. After two months he receives word that this is too expensive. At the end of his contract period Peter is completely disillusioned. He has some idea of why he has failed, but he has no one to talk to. Two days before his departure, his successor arrives full of enthusiasm. A disillusioned and frustrated Peter boards the plane for home.

Let's examine factors that may have led to this disheartening situation. Peter started an experimental garden and hired some islanders to help him with the maintenance and production. He hadn't thought to tell the population about his plans beforehand. He didn't know that a similar experimental garden had been started ten years ago, and that, for a number of reasons, this garden had also failed and had turned into a wildernis within two months. But the people still remembered this well. When he established the co-operative, Peter forgot that these people are not accustomed to doing business as a group. He didn't know that there are two political parties on the island who practice a veritable vendetta. Nor did he know that the members of the two religious groups on the island find it almost impossible to work together in a small group. He wasn't aware that the people didn't understand his stencils because they had only a few years of schooling. They would have rather bitten their tongues off than admit that they couldn't read those impressive looking papers. Peter didn't realize that the local government expected him to establish a vegetable production unit about which they could boast during the coming elections. And he found out too late that he should have sold his vegetables through the local stores.

Could Peter have done something to avoid this? Whatever the answer, one thing is certain, he wasn't fully aware of the situation, was he? The question is whether you can really blame him for anything that went wrong. Surely he could have shown some initiative by reading existing reports that he was able to find and by talking with people who had worked on the island in the past. Maybe he shouldn't have left in such a hurry, even though three years is a short time and he did want to achieve something. Why didn't the organization which sent him to the island make sure that he was better informed?

We could argue endlessly about these questions. One thing is sure, however, and that is that many of Peter's colleagues fare better, but that many have also had similar or even worse experiences. I see them often, those 'frustrated' development workers, and after talking to them one question haunts me. Did this have to happen? This question cannot be answered with a simple no. No two situations are alike and educating development workers in such a way that they become a kind of robot that can be tuned into the situation at hand is not the solution. A certain margin of freedom should be maintained for personal interpretation, adaptation and initiative. Development workers are, after all, human beings.

VOICES FROM THE FIELD

I hope I have made it quite clear that you should prepare well before starting your assignment in a developing country. The question is whether it's possible to accomplish this before departure. It's true that many organizations that send people abroad try to prepare their employees as thoroughly as possible, through courses at home and also on the job. This is a good step in the right direction, which no doubt can be further developed and improved. The question is how.

While pondering on this issue and discussing it with people who had recently returned upon termination of their contract period, I became more and more convinced that their stories and experiences are a rich source of knowledge. There's so much to learn from the experiences of people who are, at this moment, working in the field. Field workers must, of course, write periodic reports on their work and its progress. But I'm afraid that these reports are not put to much practical use. They are filed away neatly, to be only leafed through when the project is evaluated. However they are seldom used for the preparation and training of newly recruited development workers. The complaint is often heard that a development worker discovers afterwards that he has made the same mistakes in the beginning as his predecessor. This is more than just regrettable, it is a waste of human energy in a situation where energy is so vitally important. I became convinced that it would be worthwhile to let a number of these people tell their own story.

There are different ways of going about this. I decided the best approach was to visit field workers at work, with the request that they co-operate by writing an essay about their experiences. This method seemed to be the best to me because a. the purpose could be explained to each field worker individually, b. I would then have the chance to convince him that writing about his experiences is worthwhile and c. the field worker himself can in this way become more aware of the situation in which he is living and working.

Because of my professional interest in the problems of agricultural education in developing countries, the natural conclusion was that I should concentrate on issues related to the transfer of knowledge in the agricultural sector in those countries. Out of convenience I decided to approach Dutch expatriates only. During the preparatory phase, I soon discovered that most people doing this

9

kind of work are posted in Africa; they work in schools, irrigation projects, community development projects, ministeries, missions, etc. To obtain a usable list of names and addresses, I contacted several organizations that send people to developing countries with a request for names and addresses of field workers. I also included the names of several people whom I knew personally and whose contribution, in my opinion, could have been interesting. I then started corresponding with thirty of these people. These contacts were encouraging and resulted in my embarking on a long journey through Kenya, Tanzania, Zambia, Botswana, Cameroon, Ivory Coast and The Gambia. During this safari, which took approximately three months, I visited a large number of schools and projects.

Together we decided on a set of guidelines for writing the essays, based on a general outline that included a list of possible causes of initial problems. The outline was not to be considered a straight jacket, but as a memory aid and check-list. On the list a number of sources of problems were suggested, which were by no means applicable in every situation. Beginning development workers often have to deal with cultural, social, economic, theological and political, educational and project-organizational problems. In the outline the different themes were further detailed and circumscribed. This list was by no means complete. Moreover some questions were relevant in one situation but not in another. Gerrit Koeslag, one of the authors of an essay in this book, has written about beginning problems in organizing a project that involved establishing an animal husbandry training school in the north of Tanzania. He had no problems whatsoever with the characteristic relationships between men and women with which Nicolien Wassenaar was confronted in Northern Cameroon. Each writer was free to choose subjects from the outline, that applied to his own situation. The basic idea was 'if the cap fits, wear it.' This may well be the reason that very little of the original outline can be found in the essays.

I explained to them that I wanted to compile a book that would help beginners in development work, and that it was to be more a reading book than a textbook. Not a book that you have to read, but one that you want to read. A book of real-life experiences of people who try to make the best of a situation. Fortunately, the authors used their own imagination and inventiveness. The numerous letters and my journey finally reaped a harvest of eleven stories. Personally I find the stories fascinating and very educative. They give a good impression of difficulties that the authors encountered while trying to contribute to development work in the field. These are personal accounts of participants. No more and no less. Before going on to their stories, I would like to make some final comments.

A MATTER OF MEANINGS

I think that in the Netherlands, at least, people are becoming more aware of the fact that development co-operation should be based on explicit choices. Organizations that are involved in projects should continually examine the goals of their policy. This is their responsibility. But organizations are, in effect, abstractions. They are, among other things, products of individual human actions. Their policy is a resultant of the opinions and convictions of the people who are part of the organization: the governing committee and the management, but also the individual development worker who has chosen to work within this organization and thereby contribute to development co-operation. He, too, accepts a certain responsibility. He, too, can often influence the formulation of the final goals to be pursued and the ways in which these will be achieved. This implies that a development worker must be well aware of the task before him. It is not only his right, but his responsibility. He is after all responsible for his own actions.

This reasoning has its weak points, however. After all, we are dealing with human beings, with all their strengths and weaknesses. You don't always know beforehand where you'll be and what you'll be doing. That's obvious, but it doesn't relieve you of your responsibility of asking yourself whether or not you are willing to join a certain organization. Nor does it relieve you of the responsibility of finding out exactly what is expected of you in that faraway land to which you are being sent.

There are many ways of obtaining this information. I hope this book can help too. It does not say much about the broader political and economic characteristics of developing countries, but many important books have already been written about these subjects. What this book will tell you is something about what it is like to work at the grass-roots level in Africa. This way I hope to encourage you to make decisions and prepare yourself for the work you will be doing.

In 1927, A. Victor Murray, the English educator, made a journey to Africa. He boarded a boat in Genoa that brought him, via Constantinople, to Beirut. He travelled by land through the former Palestine to Port Said in Egypt. It was there that he started on an exciting expedition through the continent of Africa. He visited a large number of village schools in Kenya, Tanganyika, Rhodesia, South Africa, the Congo and West Africa. His journey stimulated him to write a fascinating book[1] called 'The School in the Bush'. His book is far more than a log of his journey. It is the well-considered contemplation of a man who was confronted with cultural situations until then unknown to him. Situations that made special demands on the Europeans who were trying to organize and stimulate education for rural people. Murray did not hesitate to examine their work critically. He did not content himself with covert racism and partially concealed feelings of superiority. Already at this early date, when colonialism still reigned, he exposed the limits of what is now called development co-operation:

> 'Culture is a matter not of things, but of meanings. The African will give his own meaning to these things when he has the opportunity of assessing them in the light of new knowledge. That is his own business. The

---

1 Murray, A. V., 1929. The school in the bush. Longman, Greene & Co., London.

business of the European is to give him of his very best and to believe that he will use it alright. The work of education consists in helping a man set up standards of judgement, and those are not always intellectual. These are not so much given to a person as – to use Pauline language – 'formed in' him, and thus education is the effect of one whole life, individual and corporate upon another whole life, individual and corporate. Life comes only from life.' (p. 336)

Eleven essays written by people working in the field now follow. There are great differences in the problems they encounter, depending on their situation. Although some minor changes have been made in the form and style of the essays, the contents have been left untouched; these are the sole responsibility of the authors.

I sincerely hope that this book will inspire development workers to adopt the spirit of Murray in their work.

2 WE FOLLOW SOMEONE WHO SPEAKS THE TRUTH

Hans Visser

WHEN THE WOODPECKER SINGS

One day our neighbour came to us. He looked very worried. The week before a woodpecker had sung near his homestead: 'tïł, tïl, tïl'. Three goats died a few days after this bad omen. The following day his mother – who was very old – passed away. The previous night the woodpecker had come again. Now his cattle seemed to be ill. The woodpecker had probably been sent by somebody who wanted to harm him. The traditional remedy is to kill a goat and to take out the stomach. The contents of the stomach, the *chyme,* are sprinkled over the whole homestead and on all stock. The chyme is a countervailing force against the evil. If this does not work, other ceremonies have to be performed, including a cursing ceremony. The person who sent the woodpecker will be cursed. He will certainly become ill and die.

The man who told us the story regularly attended our church services and requested in this case our prayers. We did not reject his story as superstitious, though it might be in our world-view. By rejecting it we would not help him. We held prayers in his homestead and we planned to get veterinary advice. The story illustrates that the world-view, including the cultural values and the religious conceptions, determine the solutions of the problems one is facing. It is therefore essential to be aware of the culture of the people one is working with.

THE POKOT

The people we stayed with were the Pokot in northwestern Kenya. They number about 150000. Most of them live in the West Pokot District, which borders on Uganda and Turkana District. The Pokot belong to the Kalenjin cluster of the Southern Nilotes. Some are pastoralists, who herd their cattle, sheep and goats in the low lying vast plains of the semi-arid and arid areas of the district. Others practise subsistence farming, especially on the slopes of the mountains, which rise to over 3000 metres and so attract far more rain. Still others have a mixed economy, keeping some animals and having small *shambas* (cultivated fields) of millet and maize. The Pokot are considered to be a very traditional and conservative people. They still wear goat and cattle skins as clothes. Their

13

houses are simple. Those of the pastoralists consist merely of branches laid on top of each other.

Their life centres around the cattle. The ideal of every Pokot is to keep animals. A man without cattle is looked upon as dead. Cattle are in the first place a means of subsistence. Blood is taken from them every month; cows are milked; oxen give meat. The Pokot make clothes, blankets and shoes from the skins. The animals play a role in social relations, notably marriage, which is not only a union of individuals but also of families. They also have great ritual value, for one needs the skin or chyme for the rituals or ceremonies. At a certain age every boy is given an ox, called a 'price-ox', about which he composes his songs and after which he is named; one is known by his ox name, which is shouted in war when one is spearing the enemy. Cattle are the object of raids on the neighbouring tribes. They are a form of legal tender and considered a mobile bank. They give a man prestige and wealth. They give him meat and clothes. They are the means for blessing and purification.

It is evident that cropping is considered secondary and additional to cattle husbandry. The cultivation of millet, finger millet, tobacco and calabashes is known. At least four varieties of millet and 20 varieties of finger millet are grown. Every farmer plants three or four varieties, which differ according to personal preference and intended use, for example food or beer. The best seeds are selected. At the same time cross-breeding (hybridization) can be achieved, because they are for 90% self-pollinating. These principles are unknowingly practised with the layout of the shambas. A hybridization effect is obtained through selecting from seeds on places where two varieties are grown. Finger millet is grown once a year, after which the land lies fallow for three years. Millet is planted throughout on the same fields, the 'shambas forever'.

Another feature of cultivation is the method of irrigation used. The water flows through hand-made channels, which can have a length of several kilometres and in which there are aquaducts and culverts. Co-operation among each other is strong, because it is necessary. The man who does not clean his part of the main channel can be fined by the community. Delta irrigation is practised in the fields.

Living as close to nature as they do, the Pokot have an intimate knowledge of the use of herbs, wild fruits and roots as food and medicines. The medicines are known and prescribed by tribal specialists, yet all Pokot have a basic knowledge about them. That is no wonder when they grow up in an environment that is experienced as harsh by us but which they consider as their home. They are therefore careful with nature. Some trees may not be cut. Some pastures cannot be used, except in times of severe droughts. They know where to find water. Still, life is hard and risky for the Pokot. Infant mortality in some areas is between 50 and 85 per cent. In an average season, half the calves will die. The irregular droughts cause famine for animals and men. The Pokot feel threatened by spiritual and magical powers. Wealth might arouse jealousy in other people. Jealousy again can be the motive to resort to witchcraft. Ritual specialists who can manipulate and foretell events by dreaming or haruspication are honoured.

15

Political power rests with the tribal elders. They are the ones who have the right to make decisions during the communal meetings. The man among them whose words have become true before is most respected – such a man is trustworthy. In their social structure they have a revolving age-set system. The age-set of the past will return in the future. With it certain events are associated; these too will recur. The Pokot is inclined to look to the past for guidance in the present. Customs, prohibitions, and values are handed on through the generations. 'It was like this in the beginning', is an often heard explanation of something. They have to be kept, because their society is built on them. One should respect the elders and follow them. Otherwise they might become angry and bring evil and misfortune upon you.

It is evident that all these factors constitute a conservative outlook of the Pokot. They are self conscious and proud of their values. As one author[1] put it: 'One feels that their way of life is inferior to none and at least equal to all'. This made our stay with them pleasant: we did not notice any feelings of inferiority towards Europeans. This does not mean, however, that no change whatsoever is taking place. Their history shows that they adopted some customs and ceremonies from other people, for example the *sapana* initiation from the neighbouring Karamojong. The most popular dance – the *adongo* – is of Turkana origin. This ceremony and this dance had a strong appeal to them, and they were spontaneously made part of their way of life.

THE POKOT AND THE EUROPEANS

In the first years of this century the policy of Pax Brittannica was extended to this part of the world. The Pokot were driven from the fertile highlands, which were divided among European settlers. But the British also halted the Turkana expansion, from which the Pokot were retreating. The District Commissioner who did this is still regarded as a hero. It is typical for the Pokot attitude that even in 1980 they say, 'The Europeans came just last night'. In their conception of time it is a recent event indeed. The traditional prophets had foretold their coming: 'One day they will come and one day they will go'.

Life did not fundamentally change with the coming of the white man. The people valued the protection against the Turkana but resented the compulsory migrations from their lands. The European court system never took root in their society. The Pokot solved their own problems in the communal meetings. Chiefs were introduced, but they never functioned well. A chief was sacked if he was weak. But he was threatened by his own people when he was strong. He had and still has an impossible function. The case of chief Kamkele of Mason illustrates this. He tried to enforce the rule that bushfires were not allowed. People grumbled when he fined them some goats. Shortly afterwards he died, allegedly

---

1   Schneider, H. K., 1959. Pokot Resistance to Change. In: Bascom, W. R. & M. J. Herskovits (Eds), Continuity and Change in African Culture. Chicago, pp. 141–167.

because of witchcraft. His successor promised to co-operate in bringing in cattle for inoculation. The next day he refused to do so, probably under pressure and because of fear of undergoing the same fate as his predecessor. He was subsequently sacked.

The missions started to work in the region in 1930. They introduced schools and started to preach the gospel. Not very many children attended. They were forced or enticed by free food. 'Why,' the Pokot asked, 'send children to school, when it is their task to herd animals?' Education of girls was rejected completely, for 'they would only learn evil things and lose the traditional values.'

'The evangelistic progress was disappointing in the extreme' according to an Annual Report of the District Commissioner in the mid-forties. Moreover the medical efforts were very slowly appreciated. In 1956 the Ortum hospital was opened by the Governor, and a medical doctor was posted there. He had to wait for six weeks, however, before the first patient could be taken in, and only then after much persuasion.

Nor did the people co-operate in land conservation and cattle inoculation. Even the department of agriculture was cursed as a 'cattle witch-doctor'. Destocking measures to preserve the land were strongly resisted. The administration became desperate about the 'illogical minds' of the people. One administrator exclaimed in 1934[1] that 'it is indeed unfortunate that a district which lends itself so easily to development should be peopled by a tribe who not only lack intelligence, but apparently any interest in their own welfare'. However around 1945 another, more enlightened, official reported[2] that 'Backwardness is not the fault of the tribe, who are in character and intelligence the equal of most and superior to many tribes, who have passed them in the race'. He said that the real reason is the fact 'that the Pokot are situated on the edge of the world'. These views are very contradictory. Is it the people or the geographical and ecological conditions that are the cause of slow development? From our perspective we can ask still another question: Is the outlook of the European administrator not the problem? Is his mind not preoccupied with concepts of civilization, development and 'uplifting', which are completely alien to the 'natives'. Such a question occurred to no one.

One European more or less gained access to the Pokot. He was G. H. Chaundy, who had an M.A. degree in agriculture and had some educational experience among the Kamba and the Maasai. He established a school in which the curriculum was heavily biased towards agriculture. Grown-up boys had to learn the 'three Rs', reading, writing and arithmetic, for two years. Work in the school garden was more important, however. He planted new crops, such as tomatoes, potatoes, maize, bananas and beans. Nine demonstration plots – spread over the district – were started. The meaning was clear: agricultural education by extension. Even after only a few years there was talk of great successes.

However Chaundy had to convince people, and words alone did not work. The

---

1   Kenya National Archives D.C., West Pokot Annual Report 1934.
2   Kenya National Archives D.C., West Pokot Report 1945.

Pokot in the more remote areas were forced to plant maize. The first time they refused, and they ate the maize seeds. They were beaten. The second time they fried the seeds before planting them; they were beaten again. Finally they consented. Their conclusion: 'Maize is not bad after all'. In an intelligence report[1] of 1936 we read the following story: 'Tribal police collected 350 people for a *baraze* (communal work). Before Chaundy began the headmen requested that the school demonstration plots be removed as the people needed no new crops. Chaundy commenced to demonstrate corn planting whereupon the women left 'en mass'. The headmen then announced that nobody wanted the government's seeds and then all the men marched away, leaving Chaundy and the District Commissioner in undisputed possession of the needed garden'. The reasons for rejection were clear to the Pokot: 'Cows might dry up'. Millet and finger millet were the traditional crops, handed down to them by the generations of the past. Why should they start with something else? The inducement of cash did not appeal to them, though Chaundy had even thought about introducing cotton.

Chaundy was reported to have the thorough confidence of the Pokot. He worked tirelessly and he claimed to have achieved more or less an agricultural revolution. That could be disputed, for only maize, and in some cases bananas, was finally accepted. Nevertheless it is no mean achievement that everything that is grown now in the district besides millet and finger millet was introduced by him in such a simple way. The rapid growth of population that the district has experienced since his days would not have been possible without this increase of acreage and diversification of crops. He was the stimulating personality behind it. His limited success was due to his personal contacts with the people, who he regularly met on his safaris. His prolonged stay of about 15 years contributed much to it, although he was too practical to penetrate deeply into the culture and the ideas of the Pokot. You may question his ethics and the method of compulsory planting, but you have to acknowledge his commitment, which was directed at the most effective level, the grass-roots. Nevertheless, even Chaundy had only a limited effect, as was shown in 1963. That year, on the instigation of a traditional prophet, the people did not plant maize at all in some areas. At the same time this incident revealed the colonial attitudes and lack of real communication and understanding of officialdom, when it described the traditional leader as a 'witch-doctor'.

THE PRESENT SITUATION OF THE POKOT

Kenya became independent in 1963. The long-awaited *Uhuru* was disappointing for the Pokot. European administrators were merely replaced by African ones. Taxes still had to be paid and destocking measures followed up. In the nation of Kenya tribal borders ceased to exist and an influx of non-Pokot, especially in the more fertile highlands, was the result. The Pokot parted easily

---

1 Kenya National Archives, West Suk Intelligence Report, 1936.

18

with their land, but in the long run tension arose between them and the 'aliens'.

The subsistence pattern really persisted. Some diversification and crop rotation showed the fruits of Chaundy's efforts. One planted maize, millet and some vegetables, but cattle continued to take first place in the hearts and the minds of the people. Cattle were the object of a flare-up of raiding and warfare between the Pokot and the Turkana that erupted in the late sixties and continued throughout the seventies. The resulting insecurity did not favour development and agricultural innovation, to say the least. This was especially true in the more remote and marginal areas.

In the seventies the major development was the building of the Great Sudan Road through the West Pokot and Turkana Districts. One of the less accessible parts of the district was opened up. More traffic, tourism, mineral prospectors, trade and even projects were the results. The modern era dawned upon the Pokot.

In the context of the Pokot's present situation the establishment of an FAO scheme at Amolem, on the border of Turkana and West Pokot, was the most impressive. The Amolem scheme was one of a cluster of similar projects along the Turkwell. These were seen as a means of rehabilitation for the Turkana, who lived in famine-relief camps after the droughts of the early sixties. Most of their cattle had been lost and people were really starving. The introduction of modern irrigation was seen as one of, if not the only, means to lessen the dependence on the relief aid. Rehabilitation was to take place through rural development. Big areas of bush were cleared, partially by hand, but largely by bulldozer. Maize and cash crops, such as sunflower, groundnuts and cotton, were introduced. People were induced to come to the projects as labourers on a 'food for work' basis. After some time they could get a plot, for which a small part of the harvest was to be handed in to pay for the costs. In 1980 about 1000 sacks of maize were harvested at Amolem, which was a considerable amount, especially as there had been a drought that year.

Although the whole system was created for the people, they had not been involved in the planning and decisions. They are more or less labourers on a farm that is run by a scheme management, in which they are only represented. The management decides what to grow and when. The idea is that the people will form a co-operative, which will eventually run the scheme. This is the only way to involve the community. The Pokot know their own irrigation projects. In this set-up, new things such as tractors and pumps have been introduced. Cash crops are being produced. Yet the Pokot traditionally do everything to produce food for their subsistence or the local market only. A co-operative has to take all these factors into consideration. The most important hindrance is that the people are not an existing community, as is the case with the traditional irrigation. They come from all parts and work together with the Turkana. The mechanization requires prolonged technical supervision and it creates a dependency on spare-parts and technical skills. Moreover the spare parts and fuel are constantly subject to price rises.

The big profits from cash crops are converted into alcoholic drink and, of course, cattle. Prostitution – unknown before – and drunkenness are the result.

Detribalization takes place. Old customs are no longer honoured, but new ones have not been found yet. The traditional system will break down in the face of the modernization. The Government is very much in favour of projects like ours. Plans have been made to plant thousands of acres with cotton and other cash crops. Tractors will be made available in the initial stages and the National Youth Service is to give a hand.

Another recent development is the goldrush. It started some two years ago, following the rise in the gold price. Several companies have obtained rights for mining. Hundreds of Pokot spend their days gold-panning in the dry riverbeds and selling their finds to the company representatives. The money is largely spent on alcohol, with its degenerating effects of fighting and neglect of the shambas. The people are liable to exploitation. This is at least in part due to the influx of so many people of other tribes, who are superior in knowledge, education and experience of modern life.

SKINS OR UNIFORMS

What can the Pokot do in such a situation? They experience the threat of famine in times of droughts. Newcomers easily compete with him for better positions. Modernization has a detribalizing effect. One day a traditional prophet told me, 'Our power is lost. Our society is becoming lost. One does not follow the elders anymore. We will be punished for it, when we send our children to school and leave the customs'.

Is this the price they should pay for development? Should they stay behind and fall easy victims to exploitation? The effects of the modern era are not to be reversed in our days. Even the international economic system in which Kenya is participating through so many links requires production and profits. All the potentials need to be developed at the fastest rate possible. No one can afford to play in the sun anymore, and to play with the Government cannot be tolerated. People therefore think that it is high time for the Pokot to throw away the skins they wear as clothes and to cut the wedding bracelet. The beads and feathers can just be set aside for public holidays. 'The Kenya we want' is, as the President of the Republic, Daniel Arap Moi, put it during his visit in 1979 to Pokot: two clean girls smartly dressed in school uniforms. They contrast with the 'Kenya, which is to disappear': two girls in skins, smeared with ochre and sheep fat. The picture of these four girls was shown to the nation in all the newspapers. The message was received by government officials at all levels: compulsory education and European clothes with immediate effect. We felt compelled to discuss these policies and to propose a grace of two years in which to teach the people to wear and maintain these clothes. In our discussion with a government official we stated that we should do things slowly to reach the hearts of the people. We were clearly told, however, not to repeat the word 'slowly' anymore, 'for we are already 1000 years behind'. This means behind the Western world.

There seems to be no way out. We Europeans have become more critical of our technological advances, our chemicals and our civilization. We feel threatened by the things we started. Africans, however, are still in the stage of unlimited admiration of technology. The gospel – and sometimes it is equated with the Gospel – is the tractor, the aeroplane and the car. The crucial question is what should you do in such a situation? What should you do as a missionary? What should you do in terms of assistance and development? Why should a volunteer lend his services for such ideals. What approach should you use if you take all these factors into consideration? We should be slow to answer these questions. The Pokot are not conservative as such. They do not reject things for the sake of rejecting them. They will not refuse new things if they do not contravene their world-view. Even their world-view and culture is adaptable. They will accept innovations when they have seen the truth of it.

OUR APPROACH

I will describe our approach to the Pokot and their situation. I will tell some stories of our encounters and experiences with the Pokot. They give me the opportunity to say something about their culture and conceptions, which influence their life. I do not pretend this constitutes a vade-mecum on how to start a project or to approach the people; many books have been written about these topics. My intention is to share some practical experiences. Some have general value, others are specifically related to the Pokot.

Get to know the people

It seems trite to start with a statement like this. And besides, everyone will say that he knows the people he is working with. Yet there are many stories to indicate the opposite. In the past expatriates have done and not done many things they wouldn't have done had they that knowledge. To know the people means to know their customs, their language, their religion and their stories. One should be able to answer the question: 'Why are they doing things in that particular way?'

My family and I spent four years among the Pokot as missionaries. We thought that we were rather close to them. Our children played with theirs, we visited them in their homes and spent a lot of time talking to each other. In our last year among them we got the opportunity to do some research on their culture and religion. We then had the role of an observer. We watched them, interviewed them and tried to learn something from them. It was indeed as if we were on a journey of discovery. Things that had occurred on the doorstep of our house became only then clear to us. We came to understand why some marriages could not be conducted, that some unions by marriage had proven to be unproductive. Before, we always believed stories about exaggerated bride prices. Then we saw the meaning of the wearing of ornaments and the colours in the ceremonies, etc. Slowly we began to see how they view those who are not Pokot, in our case the European. That view is 'slightly' different from the picture the European has made of himself. In this way one may get the right attitude. It is as St. Paul said (1 Cor. 9: 20–22), that he came 'unto the Jew as a Jew ... to them that are without the law as without the law ... to the weak as the weak ... that I might gain the weak: I am made all things to all men, that I might by all means save some'.

Let the people know you

The learning process is reciprocal. Not only should you get to know them, but the people should also get to know you just as you are. It is important to realize that Westerners are alien elements in their culture. It takes time before they can value, accept and eventually integrate them. The saying of an Pokot elder is revealing in this respect: 'We follow someone who speaks the truth'. They will see one way or the other. How can you have faith in someone if he is not true. How can somebody teach the people if he is not trusted? Is it any wonder that people resist innovations if they are proposed by people who have not yet proved their trustworthiness?

The Pokot have another conception of time than us. Our saying is, 'Time is money'. Our programme is usually full with activities. We cannot afford to waste time. We must use it efficiently. We have to achieve something. Pokot society knows nothing of these attitudes. Even their concept of time is not linear, but a cyclical, related to the cycle of age-sets. 'That what is has been and will come again'. Once I asked the opinion of some elders about the first Europeans. They said, 'They just came last night'. In our time system it was some 70 years ago! Similarly, I asked other people how they valued the work of a missionary, who had spent some ten years in the region. 'It is difficult to say', they answered, 'for he stayed so shortly with us'. This is a significant remark for us nowadays, when many development workers go out for two or three years. They feel that they have to achieve something in such a short time. We will be frustrated if we do not reach *our* targets. The people, the Africans or the Pokot, are blamed for it: no co-operation, laziness, corruption, etc. However the root of the problem is in ourselves. To know the people and to allow them to get acquainted with you is the foundation of our presence and our work. You should stay at home if you do not have the time or the opportunity for this.

The need of explanation

This heading seems, again, to be common-place. However, things are often done without a proper explanation being given. Misunderstanding and quarrels are the results of such careless actions. We were preparing a small agricultural project. It was community oriented: a project with the people, for the people and by the people. Priority was given to the growing of food – rather than cash crops. Surveys were necessary for the layout of the shambas and the irrigation canal. Marker stones were put in the field for the surveying. Rain gauges were set at several places and the water in the seasonal stream – the source of the irrigation canal – was tested. As part of the tests, salt was thrown in in large quantities.

All this was done without giving a thorough explanation to the people. Misgivings and even suspicions arose. 'Why put stones in the field? What is going to happen with our shambas? Are they going to be taken away? Why put salt in the river? Salt is food and should not be wasted. It is evil. We will be punished for it. Is our land going to be bewitched?' Finally people rejected the activities. 'We will follow our own ways. We know where they will lead us', they concluded. Proper explanations would have prevented these problems and saved this part of the project.

Taboos

Taboos might hamper development and strongly influence the people. What is our attitude, when we see through certain taboos? Taboos are on sacred places, like the pools of Ilat, the spirit of the rains. Ilat lives in the pools. In droughts animals are slaughtered near the pools to satisfy him. Sometimes pre-pubescent boys or girls are dipped into the water. People generally fear these places. Another taboo is that women should not work on an irrigation canal. Holes will appear in the canal, through which the water will run away. People say that the hole is the reflection of the vagina. There are many other taboos. Fish cannot be eaten, for they are like snakes and lizards. The warthog smells. One should not drink milk and eat meat on the same day, for the cows will dry up. This latter fear is expressed many times when something new is introduced.

We should respect these taboos as a part of the beliefs of the people. They are not our beliefs, so the taboos have no power over us. We were therefore allowed to break them if we explained it properly to the people. We ate fish and pig meat. We went to the pools of Ilat, where we asked the people's permission to swim. We were allowed, but the risk was ours. On one occasion the people stood in awe as we went into the water, expecting lightning and thunder from the enraged Ilat. Nothing happened. On the way home we were surprised by showers of rain. The conclusion of the people was that going into the water was for us not bad. Ilat favoured it, for he benevolently blessed us afterwards with rains. We broke the taboo, but we cannot force the people to do the same. However, by our actions we show something that eventually will be regarded as truth.

Value their knowledge

People who manage to survive in the harsh conditions there have an intimate knowledge of nature, of which they are so much a part. This can be a treasure and even a source of wisdom, for we can learn various things from them. For instance, about herbs. They know of hundreds of herbs and roots that can be used to cure various diseases of animals and men. The interest shown by organizations like the WHO recognizes this fact. The same is true of the nutritious value of wild fruits, roots, etc. The Pokot have managed to stay alive through their knowledge of these things. The people are also skilled in preparing skins and carving. Among them are skilled blacksmiths and potters. Their knowledge and the skills will disappear in the face of encroaching Western civilization.

In Pokot social life special attention is paid to the position of the women. 'She' is seen with two other bodies: the husband and the child. It is said that Venus will urinate after she has lain with her husband. It means that it will rain. There are many other examples of their practical knowledge and experience. To ignore this would be harmful to all parties.

Explore the existing potentials

There are potentials in the traditional economy. For example, all Pokot are fond of honey, which can be found in trees, caves and in the soil. There are different types of bees that produce the honey. Nearly all Pokot have beehives, which they make themselves. They know the good trees in which to put them. One *pachon* can have 25–30 hives. He might collect an average of five containers, which is at least 20 kg, a month. This could already provide a living for a family. Much could be achieved if one used this potential. There is room for improvement through management and marketing. Similarly, there will be other potential resources in animal husbandry and agriculture.

Work through the community structures

Many development projects are community-oriented; the communities should be the bearers of the projects. Communities do not need to be formed, they already exist. Irrigated agriculture was and is conducted by the whole community. All are interdependent upon one another for the clearing of the channels. Agreements about who may use the water, and when, are made. It is just one example of how a community is running its own affairs. Development could and should be channelled through these existing communal structures. On this point it is important to differentiate between the power structure and the social structure of a community.

The power structure consists of the elders of the community. The real authority concerning every sphere of life is vested in the elders. They have also ritual powers, which give them even more respect. The chief, headman or any government representative, cannot do anything without their approval and co-operation. Things need to be discussed with them. One has to make sure that a project is accompanied by their blessings before it is started.

Social structures have to be taken into account as well. They are affected by development. The small agricultural project already mentioned provides an example. We thought it wise to divide the area in equal plots for the men, as heads of the homesteads. We did not consider, however, that many of them were polygynous: they have several wives and consequently several families. It was argued that a man with more wives needed more land, as his families needed more food. The counter argument was that the mission could not sanction polygyny in this way. Furthermore, it would mean that the existing inequality would be strengthened if plots of different sizes were handed out. One man could for instance claim three units, while another got only one!

The traditional society is based on polygyny. In fact it is necessary in a society that has more women than men. Every woman in Pokot society should produce children. This is done in a polygynous structure. Every wife of a polygynous household gets from her husband a plot to grow millet or maize. This shamba should provide enough food for her and her children. A discussion about the polygyny as an institution and the missionary attitude against it is out of place in this context. The same is true of a discussion about inequality. One cannot transform the structures of society inmmediately through an agricultural project, although higher production will have an effect on the structures of the society in the long run. Polygyny is disappearing rapidly in the more 'advanced' areas of Africa. There are higher standards of living and there is better sanitation. This will bring down the birth rate generally and the surplus of women as well. Many factors play a role here and it is of vital importance to take them all into account.

Small is beautiful

Projects and innovations should be initiated at the grass-roots level, and then only on a small scale. The reasons are obvious. Innovations should be accepted and assimilated by the people themselves. They have therefore to be introduced at their level, within their comprehension. If the innovation is accepted and assimilated, it will automatically become a part of their way of life. The innovation will regenerate itself. Take the case of Chaundy: maize was finally accepted and it is now considered by the Pokot as indispensable. Many attempts were made to start cotton and groundnut schemes. They all failed, because they were initiated without the direct involvement of the people and on too big a scale. As such, they could not be assimilated by the Pokot. Personal contacts at the grass-roots level will stimulate development more than anything else.

Development is not to be imposed

A proper understanding of development excludes imposition. Development means growing and self-generating. Nevertheless, experiences with compulsory education and compulsory maize planting show that others have not always been afraid to impose something when persuasion did not work. We impose too, in a more subtle way, when we only make funds available for projects that we consider viable. We refuse to initiate some and accept others. It is decided by us, not the people.

On one occasion all leaders of the district had a meeting about development. The District Officer raised the idea that the Pokot could do well rearing chickens and that co-operatives should be formed. Pokot should be known as chicken land. The Pokot in the meeting did not show much enthusiasm. That stimulated the officer only to talk louder and to prolong his speech. Finally everyone agreed, unwillingly, to the plan. Co-operatives should be formed. The Pokot would have a bright future with their chickens. Nothing happened, however, as could easily have been predicted. Most Pokot dislike chickens, for they are birds; they refuse to eat the eggs.

Things that are imposed are rejected, if not in words then certainly in attitude or actions, and even rituals. The government might in these cases even be viewed as an enemy to be defeated. The same applies to missionaries and other volunteers who press their point too much. The traditional prophet will tell the people what to do to get rid of such an undesirable element.

Value the rituals

Rituals will be carried out to prevent the spread of a disease or to drive it off, when it attacks man, animal or plant. A well-known ceremony of the Pokot that we have witnessed is the *Karera*. The millet and maize had been eaten by the army-worm. One morning nine girls – naked but for the ashes smeared over their bodies – went like warriors through the fields. They collected stalks from the diseased plants. Some of the worms were taken to the house of ants to be eaten by them. A number of ritual actions were carried out with the stalks. It highlighted in the cursing of the worm. All the women closed their eyes and said:
> 'Go without production.
> Go without blowing
> Go without waste.
> Wife of a worm.'

The crow, the meat-eating bird, the vulture, the rat, the bush-baby, the squirrel, the porcupine, the warthog, the baboon, the wild pig, the hyrax and the monkey were all called upon to destroy the worm. They really believe that these words will be carried out by some supernatural power, which might be God. Our method of dealing with the army-worm is to use chemical pesticides, which are probably more effective. We do not pay attention to the magical dimension. We treat it objectively. For us it is no subject to address, but an object that we destroy. Yet we should not have the illusion that the magical dimension has disappeared from the lives of the Pokot. And it continues to play a role. We should not neglect this underlying belief nor underestimate its role. For instance, there is a ceremony in which shambas are closed ritually, but effectively: nobody is allowed to pass through, which prevents the spread of contagious diseases.

We face in this a whole set of problems that I can only indicate here. It is the confrontation of a culture in which the magical-religious component is intertwined with a culture in which technology, sophistication and secularization are predominant. The crucial question is whether they are mutually exclusive or not. Africans cannot understand that there are people who do not believe in God or supernatural powers, and there are Westerners who can only laugh at their rituals. Problems are likely to arise through such interactions and confrontations. An approach that only pays attention to some aspects of life and neglects others will reduce the wholeness of man. We see the fruits of these developments in our Western culture. We have therefore to take man and his world view seriously, in all his relations and in all his needs. I believe that the deepest confrontation takes place for all of us in the Lord Jesus Christ. This meeting takes place in every area of life, including agriculture and animal husbandry.

EPILOGUE

I have outlined some problems that are besetting 'development' among the Pokot. Their cause is put down to lack of understanding of their culture and their world-view, or in other cases to lack of real involvement of the Pokot people. Yet development is important for them. The Pokot have to participate in the modern era or they will cease to exist.

I believe we should take time to listen to the Pokot to avoid the pitfalls. We should evaluate ourselves. Who are we? What are we doing? The optimism of the development era of the sixties has gone. Things are not as easy as we thought. Ideology and practice showed too much discrepancy. In fact, life in many parts of Africa is more difficult now than it was twenty years ago. Experts fear widespread famines in the coming years if the pattern of agriculture is not changed.

At the same time the problems at home – energy, recession, environment – have made us more modest about transposing our systems elsewhere. Things are not as simple as we thought. However these considerations should not prevent us from becoming involved in the problems and to help those without a helper. Let us look at the whole of man's needs. The study of culture will help us in this respect. Let us not only go as teachers to other people, but also as students. It will benefit them and us.

3 SETTLING NOMADS; FIGHTING A LOSING BATTLE?

Gerrit Noordam

ABOUT HUNTERS AND HERDERS

Loyapat is located on the river Wei-Wei, on the boundary of the Turkana and Pokot areas, in the northern part of the Rift Valley Province in Kenya. The main objective of the project in which I am working is to make the people from this area and others staying in 'famine refuge camps' self-supporting by trying to get them to settle and cultivate the land. Only part of this arable land is available now; the rest is to be reclaimed. There are complementary projects to provide buildings for schools and dispensaries, and for missionary activities. This project was begun in 1973. By the end of 1980 an area of 60 acres was being cultivated and irrigated within a surface irrigation system. At present 60 families have a plot. The project is sponsored by the Dutch Reformed Church and the Dutch Government.

The Turkana people are by origin pastoral nomads. Turkana District is about twice as big as the Netherlands and has 200 000 inhabitants. Because of droughts many families have lost their animal herds (camels, cows, goats and sheep); they are called *maskini*. Since the early seventies different settlement schemes have been started. Some under the aegis of FAO. Others have been initiated by different churches.

Loyapat is located at a place where some Turkana people already used to live. They managed to survive on what was growing near the river and some rainfed crops they cultivated. Their main interest was and still is hunting, however. Most of them have asked for an irrigated field, but that is because legally they are not allowed to hunt anymore. Maskini and hunters have been thrown together in five different camps at Loyapat. There are also about 50 maskini living in our camp who are not able to cultivate a plot because they are too old or handicaped. They are given food daily. These people have a very marginal place within the family structure. After they have been helped for some years, it is difficult to put them again under the care of their original family.

Education is obligatory in Kenya. However, only 78% of the children on our scheme attend school (at the end of 1980). The school provides education up to Standard V, and every afternoon adult-literacy classes are held. Some school buildings are still under construction. They are meant to be permanent, which means that they are built from cement blocks and roofed with corrugated iron sheets. None of the present teachers are Turkana. Only two out of the six teachers are married. They are all living on the school compound, close to the class-rooms.

The different problems we are facing in this project are not only being dealt with from an educational point of view, other aspects are being considered as well, especially the settlement. This settlement scheme is an irrigation scheme in a nomadic area of the Turkana District. This district has been administered for only the last 20 years. Therefore, this project is facing some special problems.

NO UNIFORM, NO SCHOOLING

The children of Loyapat went to school for the first time in 1974. About 30 per cent of them, aged between 7 and 14 years, began in Standard I. Of that group only two pupils have reached Standard VII. Most pupils leave the school when they are 14 years or older. Also, this year we lost about five pupils from Standards II and III. They went to small gold-mining areas in the district. Some parents refuse to bring their children to school. They either do not see the benefit of education or they simply need the children to take care of their goats.

Some parents do not allow their children to put on Western clothes, in this case the school uniform; they prefer that they continue to wear their skins. We have no problem with them wearing skins but the Kenyan government does not tolerate children wearing these clothes during classes. The children get a uni-form when they come to school, but because they then wear it day and night the uniforms are worn out after only a few months. The parents have no money to buy clothes for their children, so many children come naked to school after their uniform is worn out. The mission does its best to supply them with some second-hand clothes. For pupils, it is impossible to do any homework, because almost no Turkana family has a petrol-lamp. Moreover none of the parents can stimulate or help their children. This means that pupils have to depend entirely on themselves. They have to find money, clothes, and everything else needed for them to go to school. The school does provide food, because in most families food is very scarce.

We have about five children at the school whose parents are not at Loyapat. There are also six or seven pupils without parents and some others have only a mother or a father. In total there are about 100 pupils. Every year the conditions for our pupils are improving a little bit, but for quite a number of them life is still very difficult. There are practically no possibilities for them to go to secondary school or any other schools. There are only two secondary schools in Turkana and hardly any other schools, and there is no money for travel to other districts. Only five pupils of those who finished Standard IV in 1979 went to other mission schools.

PROJECT STAFF AND LOCAL TEACHERS

The present teachers are not Turkana. These teachers are paid by the government, although three of them are on the project's pay-roll. When all

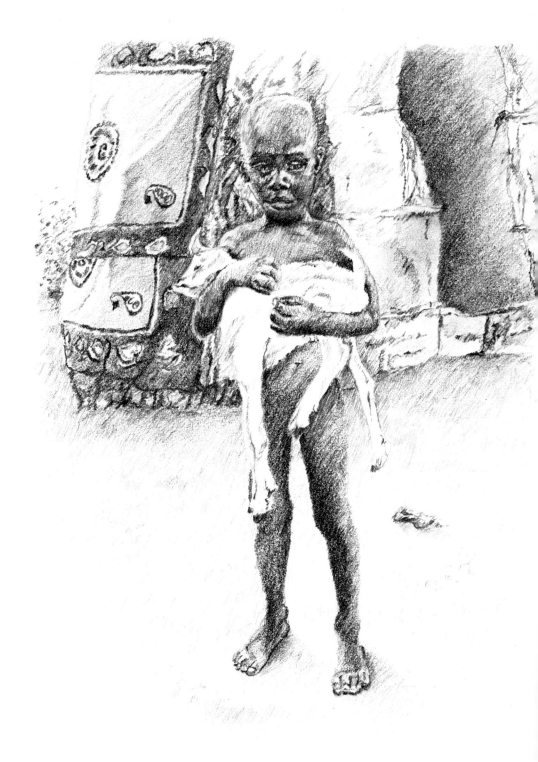

buildings are completed, around 1983, the school will be handed over to the government. The school should be a full primary school by that time, teaching Standards I to VII.

There is quite a difference in motivation among the teachers. Some are only teaching to draw a salary, while others see their work as 'helping and developing Turkana'. These people are willing to do some voluntary work.

The school is not only sponsored but also managed by the project staff. This possibly has an influence on the level of absenteeism of teachers, which is very low compared with other schools in this area. Also, teachers generally return on time after their leave. (The system here is three months school, one month holiday) Our teachers do not speak the Turkana language. This can be a disadvantage, especially in the first classes. Children seem to learn Swahili quite easily, however.

Local teachers do take good care of themselves. The scheme has given a one-acre plot to the school on which to grow vegetables for the children. But many things that are grown are eaten by the teachers. It is very difficult to stop this practice.

Contacts between the management and the teaching staff are rather good, probably in part because the school is fully dependent on the project sponsors for equipment, transport and allowances. It is preferred that the teaching staff bears its own responsibility for the rules of education, the level of learning and so on. The project staff are only there to stimulate and guide. There is a special need to stimulate the involvement of the community in the different activities of the school

SCHOOL AND COMMUNITY

Most problems that concern the children and the relations between school and parents find their source in the family and community structure, and in cultural background. As the Loyapat community consists of families coming from different places, no clear community structure has crystallized out as yet. This implies a lack of social control and authority, which also spills over into parent-child relationships. It seems to be very difficult for the parents to organize their present way of living and regain authority over their children. Moreover the distance between parents and children is growing, because the children are beginning to perceive their parents as illiterate and old-fashioned. In this way pupils are becoming disoriented. Obviously the school has to replace the parents partly, but at the same time it must try to bring parents and children together again, through activities such as home visits, parents' days, school committees with community representatives and adult literacy courses. So far, however, it seems that the school is pulling children away from their parents and their Turkana traditions.

The project manager and the project staff have to follow the educational system wanted by the Kenyan government. At the same time, however, they are expected to stimulate processes and systems that can be to the benefit of the

31

whole community. Sometimes these two functions clash. When working together with teachers, parents and other members of the scheme, the project staff sometimes faces special difficulties.

The project staff was heavily blamed by the teachers when it proposed that children without a uniform could come to school in their traditional clothes. If parents had no money to buy Western clothes, the teachers said, the school should provide the necessary clothes; the teachers thought this should be paid by the project sponsors.

IT IS NO USE GOING NATIVE

Finding appropriate housing can be a big problem. When I arrived in Africa I had to complete some courses and make some orientation trips. After that you really feel like settling down and starting your work and a normal family life with your wife and children. In our case we didn't get a chance to settle down. We moved from a grasshouse to a semi-permanent house, and then after a year to a permanent house. Housing is really important because of the climate, insects and wildlife, and for security reasons. At Loyapat it is too hot for our children to play outside, which means that there has to be some space to play inside the house. Our children cannot go to school because of problems with language. For our family it was a real improvement to be able to move to a permanent house. The only disadvantage is the difference in standard of housing compared with that of the local people, but fortunately this is no obstacle for our good contacts. It is also very important to have clean water; we dug some wells to get that. Those wells also provide the community with water, so there are less cases of disease and diarrhoea.

In my opinion the house should be placed a bit outside the centre of the community to allow some privacy. It is not easy to take a break here because people think you are on duty 24 hours a day. To prevent difficulties it is good to have your office far from your house. Since people are extremely poor you can expect them to come to ask for a personal loan or some other sort of material assistance. They often come to my house on non-working days or after working hours. People can come for food and sit in front of your door the whole day. It is good to have certain family rules on how to deal with this, but each family will solve this problem differently. We try to build up a good system of relationships, but we help people mostly through the project office. It is also very important to try to teach people to save a little money or the farmers to save or store crops. The savings may be deposited in the project office.

The building of houses for project workers will depend on the funds allotted, the availability of different materials and the preferences of the people concerned. A permanent house of cement blocks and an iron roof was built for a staff member; the total cost was about KSh 20000. Now he is asking for a grasshouse (which are built presently for other project workers); such a house costs only KSh 4000. He wants a grasshouse because it is much cooler and is more fitted to his personal needs. Before starting to build, it is a good idea to find out what the new residents expect in terms of living facilities.

Transport is available. The only difficulty is that this project is 10 kilometres from a mainroad and can only be reached by a private road. There is a project car for transporting goods, sick people and so on. Having transportation does make it necessary to have a well-controlled system to prevent the vehicle being misused. Goods like spare-parts and food must be bought in a town 225 kilometres away. Our families – there is another expatriate family on the project – go about every six weeks to shop there. The road has been greatly improved but it is still an uncomfortable trip, especially when travelling with small children. Because of the bad quality of the roads, travelling can be dangerous too. There are always so many people who would like to travel with you. Mostly it is nice but sometimes I feel irritated about it, after all, I am not a taxi-driver.

So there are some economic and material difficulties, but most problems are much more connected with the efficiency of the development organization you are working for (salary, car, house, etc.), the country and region you are living in, and the people you are living with. For example, as far as we have noticed here, it is no big problem for the local people in the project that we have another life-style than theirs, with our many material facilities.

ADJUSTED PROJECT MANAGEMENT, NO BLUEPRINT

As this project is sponsored by two different institutions, sometimes financial and organizational difficulties arise. This is mostly due to difficulties in communication. Distances are long and letters can be easily misinterpreted. I have already said that this project has its special features. It needs, therefore, flexible and efficient guidance. 'Knowhow' has to be co-ordinated properly to carry out an effective planning procedure. Some technical, social and other studies have been done for the project, but the results have never been compared and discussed with the donors. The problems concerning the internal project organization are strongly related to backstopping.

It is necessary to draw up a proper budget for the school for the coming year. It is important that the local staff participates in planning, management and budgetting. Too often the people concerned do not know anything about the objectives, the planning or the financial side of their project. The same applies for this project. We have to try and change this situation as quickly as possible.

One of the most important aims of an agricultural project of this kind should be to stimulate self-reliance. This can only be done when all people in the project are informed, involved and given more and more responsibility. It is very difficult to make the people understand that the help given in this settlement scheme is only for a few years. They think that the mission has started the scheme to help them cultivate a piece of land, not only for now but also in the future. The whole idea that they must become self-reliant in a few years is completely strange to them. It is even difficult to make this clear to the local scheme staff. The whole project-organizing structure should aim to create systems in which the people involved are compelled to take more responsibility.

Another aspect of project management is personnel. One of the project aims is to employ Turkana people where at all possible. Sometimes it is difficult to make a choice, especially as there are always many applicants. Some jobs have been created just to give employment to as many people as possible, especially the maskini. It is quite easy to get some qualified people from other tribes, as there are about 13 non-Turkana in the project area. Sometimes this causes quarrels, but all of them do their job properly.

> The agricultural adviser has a difficult job. When he helps the farmers a bit with the digging or cleaning of a canal or by showing them how to hold a spade they often conclude that he is most fitted for that kind of work, and they just leave to hunt. When they are given seeds for planting they sometimes just eat them (especially groundnuts). The advisor's suggestions on planting, top-dressing and crop rotation are often neglected.

Applications for leave and travelling allowances also create difficulties. The distance to the nearest town is approximately 225 km and there are no taxi's or buses on the road. This means that people can be away for two or three days just to collect a single identity card. And then they might be asked to come back next week . . . This creates irritation, costs money and delays work. It can also be difficult to decide when somebody asks for two, three or more weeks leave because of problems in the family. It is not always possible to check the truth of the different stories; in such cases I find it particularly useful to involve the staff, because they will often know the background and private circumstances of the man concerned.

For all these matters you have to develop some feeling. It is useful to make good private contacts with the people you are working with, after working hours. Do not be too afraid to visit the local people, try to learn how to play their games or go out together on excursions. Problems of organization depend on many aspects, but they have all to be seen in relation to the specific circumstances in the project or school.

THE TONGUE OF MAN IS A TWISTY THING

In the beginning it was difficult to communicate with the people, but with enough patience this improves daily. It is very important to start speaking with the people, even when you only know a few words. Mostly the people take you seriously and respect it when you try to learn their language. In this project it was a bit difficult in the beginning because only the staff is able to speak English. Almost 70 per cent of the Turkana speak Swahili, which is the most important language in Kenya. It is very important to learn this language. Because they speak it in an easy way I can communicate, at least on a low level. To do a good job here, it also is a great benefit to speak the Turkana language. But it is almost impossible to learn as the language is very difficult and has not yet been expressed in writing. I only know the most important greetings, which is already very useful. As mentioned it is problematic when there are no Turkana teachers in school, especially for communications between teachers and parents. Perhaps it does have one advantage: the pupils are forced to learn Swahili very quickly.

WORKING WITH DILEMMAS

As I am here to do some missionary work as well, it is necessary to know a bit of local religion. It is quite important for any development worker to know something about local beliefs. In the working situation, I have not yet faced any important difficulties because of their beliefs. In this scheme many aspects of local beliefs and habits have changed and still are in a process of transformation. It is a problem but also a challenge to find out how these changes can be guided and used in the settlement scheme to the benefit of all participants.

The real difficulties arise on the medical side of things. It often happens that traditional treatment and modern treatment conflict. It is a local medical practice that older people try to get power over a patient's illness. The patient often follows the advice of such a person because their traditional treatment is strongly rooted in culture and religion. In our dispensary we often have patients who have been treated locally. Apparently the treatment did not help, for they are brought to our clinic. Sometimes, however, when our medicines do not give any relief, local treatment is sought. When people give local medicines to the patients it often helps. On other occasions, when treating serious diseases, the local healers start cutting the body because they contend that something is wrong with the blood and that it has to be drained. This is a method that is still very usual here; although it sometimes helps, it causes deaths too. The only thing I can say is that we are too ignorant about this aspect of local culture.

It could be very important to have some kind of democratic system within a project so that the people can air their opinions and make suggestions. For our project it is also necessary to have at least some Turkana in the project staff. Despite such democratic provisions the project staff is sometimes forced to act like a little dictator. It is good to have many different ideas but it can easily frustrate the daily management of the scheme.

THE DAILY 'BREAD'

At first, we did not understand how people were able to feed themselves. Later on, especially when we met people in their houses in the bush, we began to understand, for we noticed that they not only eat maize. Traditionally the Turkana people consume milk, meat and blood, but not much else. Now, here on the scheme the group of hunters has adapted already to eat all kind of fruits, vegetables, meat and, especially, honey. For the maskini it is no problem to eat maize and vegetables. When these are scarce, however, they have no alternative food sources. When a hunter neglects his plot there is no food problem; even his wife and children know how to 'survive'. But if the maskini do not till the soil they will suffer, their wives and children especially; the man can always join the hunters. Then there is a real problem: what to do about it when these women and children are starving? Should we give food to these families? No, because then they will never work their fields again. Remove the man from his plot? No, because then they have to be taken to the 'famine relief' project. The only way is to talk and to try to stimulate the man to go back to his field. This is exactly the main problem on this project.

We do not have any problems with our own food supply. Everything necessary is available in this country. The only thing is that the nearest town is quite far from our camp.

TEACHER TAKE YOUR TIME!

Most of the teachers in our school do not know anything about didactics. Most of them have had only primary school and some years of secondary education. Only one of them has finished a teachers' training college. This means that compared with Western education, the didactic aspects are neglected. Yet we are very much in need of inventive and flexible teachers, because we have a very short supply of teaching aids, for example books and materials. The teacher must organize the whole process of learning all by himself, so he needs to be well-trained. The aim of this school is to teach the children the most elementary subjects, such as reading, writing, Swahili and English, and to reach the desired standard (level) of primary education as soon as possible. Thus it is very important that the character of training given in teacher training colleges be adapted to the situation in remote regions, like the Turkana District. I know that the Turkana District is considered by most teachers as the worst of places to go to. They are not very motivated to do everything possible to develop education here. This too could possibly be improved by changing and extending the preparatory phase of young people who express the wish to make a career in teaching.

However it is possibly good when things are improving only slowly. There is no need to do everything in a hurry. It took a long time before a good school system was functioning in Europe, and even now there are many problems to solve. Our school has already achieved some remarkable results and we should be grateful about that.

As far as farming is concerned it seems to be more difficult to change things. Some problems have been explained. We have tried to do our best to improve motivation but so far we have not succeeded much. Although some things are improving a bit, we have already learned that we have to be very patient. One or two people cannot enforce change, they must motivate the people to change. To do so they must take full account of the social, cultural and economic context these people are living in. It takes a lot of time.

4 FROM SISAL ESTATE TO DAIRY TRAINING CENTRE

Gerrit J. Koeslag

GENESIS OF A PROJECT

Through the efforts of a Dutch expert in Tanzania, working with the Tanzania Rural Development Bank, a team of two Dutch experts in practical training in dairying went to Tanzania in early 1978. In collaboration with two Tanzanian officers of the Ministry of Agriculture they investigated the feasibility of establishing a centre for practical training in dairying somewhere in Tanzania. At the same time they identified the need for this type of training and the persons who had to be trained (target groups).

This type of practical training is unknown in Tanzania. The Dutch members of the identification mission said in their letter that accompanied the mission report:

> 'Apart from the choice where to establish the centre, the lack of knowledge of this type of practical training in Tanzania caused problems when fixing the duration of courses/programmes; the number of trainers/instructors and the expenses for the training'.

The reason behind introducing this type of training in Tanzania was that the large-scale dairy farms, established as part of the Dairy Development Plan Phase I, financed by the World Bank, showed many problems. One of these problems was a lack of practically-trained staff of all levels.

The Tanzanian-Dutch mission visited several regions in Tanzania where dairy farming could have possibly been introduced or extended. After considering potential locations it chose the Tanga region. Although this region has less favourable points for the development of dairy farming – it is tse-tse infested and there is no real 'history' of dairy cattle husbandry – there were enough strong points to establish the centre there. Ultimately the decision was a political one rather than a technical-economic one.

The mission recommended that the centre for practical training in dairying should comprise:
– accommodation and facilities for students/trainees that enable practical training in dairy farming (infrastructure, classrooms, offices, a students' hostel, etc.).
– a farms section, consisting of a large-scale, a medium-scale and small-scale dairy farm. The total proposed area was 800 hectares, of which 400 hectares was to be cultivated immediately.

Apart from the training task of the farms section, this section should also produce milk, since the policy of the Tanzanian government is that the regions become self-sufficient in milk production. The maximum number of students/trainees was set at thirty-two; the number of students/trainees per 'practice' group was not to exceed eight. Allowance was also made for an increase in the number of students/trainees in the future.

The duration of the bilateral co-operation between the governments of the United Republic of Tanzania and the Kingdom of the Netherlands for this training centre was fixed at five years, an unusually long agreement; projects are in general limited to two or three years. However I do believe that this longer commitment of the two governments is much more favourable than a short duration project. A possible extension of three years was allowed for as well.

A Dutch team of experts would assist the Tanzanian staff in implementing and operating the training centre. The team would consist of a project teamleader, who at the same time would be deputy principal, a senior trainer/instructor and a farm manager.

This account is limited to social, economic-material and project-organizational problems because the project has not as yet reached the point that other sources of problems can be discussed: the project is still in an initial phase, apart from the farms section, which is partly in operation.

EXPERT AND HUMAN BEING

Being an expert

I was selected by DTH[1] as the project teamleader. Despite the comprehensive job description for my position I have been amazed over the past year to find how little my knowledge and experience in practical training is valued. I have sometimes even had the idea that they are a disadvantage. I regret that some of my plans and suggestions have been considered as overdone or not feasible, although in my opinion they were absolutely correct in view of the teaching/training aspects. This stance of DGIS's is surprising because it has quite some problems in recruiting qualified experts to staff its development projects in several countries. Creating disappointment and even frustration among its expatriate experts will hardly improve the situation.

Fighting the paper tiger

The regulations and legislation for purchasing land by a government institution are quite complicated. In many ways it is a kind of a challenge to find out

1   DTH = Directie Internationale Technische Hulp van het Ministerie van Buitenlandse Zaken (Technical Assistance of the Ministry of Foreign Affairs); DTH has been reorganized as DGIS = Directoraat Generaal Internationale Samenwerking (Development Co-operation Department).

how it works, but it can be very frustrating too: one day you think you have discovered one thing to be true, only to discover the next day the opposite.

I arrived in Tanga in 1979, in the second half of October. I was disappointed to see that no land was available to establish the training centre. The acquisition of the land had already begun, but it took another three months before the whole affair had been settled.

I also had to get to know some of the labour laws and regulations, because we employ a large number of labourers. If you are not aware of the rules you can easily run into problems. For example, if formal mistakes are made when labourers are hired or let go, this can lead to – justified – complaints. In spite of all our efforts labourers sometimes bring charges against us. Although all this might be unavoidable it consumes a lot of time, which could be better used for project-oriented activities. Without taking the trouble of looking into these regulations and laws it would be quite difficult to understand some actions taken by the casually or permanently employed labourers.

Understanding the world of work

It might sound a bit strange to mention this in an account of the problems of a teacher in a developing country, but I can assure that everybody is confronted with this issue sooner or later. The conditions under which the labourers have to work are different to those in most Western European countries. From a social point of view the labourers are well protected by the labour laws and regulations, but from a climatic and economic point of view labourers are not well off. The climatic conditions are particularly hard (heat and high humidity). Their wages are rather low when one takes in account the ever-rising prices. Even for us expatriates it is difficult to decide whether to buy certain food stuffs or not because they are extremely expensive. Although prices are fixed by the government, black-market prices openly prevail. In my opinion one of the reasons why labour productivity is not very high is because the diets of the labourers are limited in quality and quantity. If they are not well fed they tend to need to rest more.

I was initially surprised to see how staff of various levels make use of project vehicles and equipment. They seem to expect that these materials may be used for private purposes at random. Although it is against government regulations to use government and parastatal vehicles for private purposes you see them regularly after office hours, apparently in use as private vehicles. I think this must be costing the Tanzanian government a lot of money as it is already extremely difficult to keep even the normal transport going (including government transport), because of shortage of tyres, spare-parts and very high fuel prices.

Working with the counterpart

By my first job description, I was to be the teamleader of the Dutch team of experts and at the same time deputy principal of the institute. This is a situation I cannot recommend. As a teamleader I am responsible for the contribution of the government of the Netherlands to the project, and for implementation of the entire project. Yet should a dispute arise with the Tanzanian principal who has the final say, me or him? A similar situation exists for other expatriates on Dutch bilateral projects. They are not answerable to Tanzanians, for example, only to the teamleader. As no official project agreement has been drawn up, this change in responsibilities and authority could be introduced rather easily.

My counterpart and I are still gauging each others points of view and opinions. Immediately after his appointment as the principal, my counterpart went to the Netherlands to follow a course to get acquainted with all the special ins and outs of practical training as it is practised in the Netherlands. Most probably this is one of the reasons that our relations, perhaps it is more accurate to say our ability to communicate with each other along the same lines, is a bit strained. For I worked without my counterpart for some months while he was away and that could have led to the situation in which I easily take the lead-rein and act on my own insights. In addition to this, the principal, wisely, acts with care because he feels he is no expert in practical training as yet. As a result he does not very often oppose proposals and ideas brought forward by the Dutch team of experts. However, I think that with time this situation will certainly improve.

Due to family affairs . . .

Although they do not have much to do with the real task for which I came to Tanga, private events can have a very big influence on one's ability to work. The first unhappy event came quite soon after our arrival. My wife discovered she had a small tubercle in her breast. Our doctor advised us to have her return to the Netherlands to investigate whether or not it was harmless. We decided she should go alone and that I should stay with our three children, who had to attend school. Depending on the results of the medical tests, we would stay or return to the Netherlands. After a week of great tension and loneliness I was informed that the tumour had been removed and was harmless. My wife returned safely to Tanzania; the whole affair took less than three weeks.

We were one year in Tanzania when we received the message of the unexpected death of my mother-in-law. Although we knew she was a heart patient we did not expect it at all, because the day before the message reached us, we received a letter saying 'no problems' and extending her very best wishes to us all. We all returned to the Netherlands, although this was not an easy decision to make: our children had to attend school and at that moment I was the only Dutch expert at the project, because the team was not complete. However as it turned out we are very happy to have witnessed the burial, although upon our return to Tanga we were all quite broken and very tired. At that very moment we began to realize what had happened and what it meant for the future: no visits to mother and grandmother anymore. It was some time before we overcame this blow.

MAKE YOURSELF AT HOME

A Dutch touch

Although a large difference exists in the financial capabilities of the Dutch expert in comparison with his Tanzanian counterpart, let alone other Tanzanians, the difference in life style is not as large as one might expect. I think that the Tanzanians have other priorities than us. They give priority to social life: more contacts in the street, visits to bars, etc. We prefer to stay at home and to make that the centre of our social life. I believe this might even be considered as a typical Dutch touch, because in my job in the Netherlands foreign students at my college noticed it as well. In general we like to furnish our homes as comfortably as possible. But Tanzanians do not have very many opportunities to do so, because almost all luxury items, like refrigerators, deep-freezers and good quality furniture, are not, or only sometimes, available, and then only at very high prices. Basic foodstuffs such as sugar, flour, maize and rice, and other products, like soap, are regularly in short supply. In general they are not sold at the prices fixed by the government. This implies that Tanzanians have to spend a high percentage of their income on basic foodstuffs.

Although many luxurious goods and foodstuffs are not available I feel that we need less here than in the Netherlands. Moreover we feel less social pressure from our neighbours than we might in the Netherlands. In spite of the fact that you try to escape a certain comparison with neighbours or friends with respect to your way of life, it still happens in the Netherlands. The social life in the family circle is better here because there are less commitments and less influences from outside, like television.

A house is not a home

When we arrived in Tanzania we were expecting to have to live in a hotel for only a few days before we could move into one of the staff houses on the project. Unfortunately there was no house and we had to stay almost six weeks in a hotel. This was not a very convenient place for our children to do their homework or have a good rest. The daily regime in a hotel does not ensure that. Moreover the dispatch of our personal belongings had been delayed because of strikes in Rotterdam harbour and, to cap it all off, part of the belongings we sent by air had been stolen.

We finally succeeded in renting a house through our own efforts. We had lived there only three weeks when the owner sold the house to a steel factory, which had plans to accommodate senior staff in it. Because the official documents for renting the house had not been completed, we had no legal basis to stay.

At that time it was difficult to find accommodation in Tanga and we had not found alternative accommodation before we had to vacate the house. From that moment on, once or twice a week a representative of that steel factory came to remind us that we were illegally occupying the house. He threatened to throw us out of the house – if necessary by force. I still believe that they did not

42

dare to do this because I was an expatriate, working on a development project. Anyway, the whole situation was embarrassing, particularly for my wife as she mostly had the pleasure of receiving our 'visitor'. Then we entertained a hope of getting one of the staff houses on the project, because the land had been purchased by the Ministry of Agriculture. But we were again disappointed because the occupants were allowed to stay there.

At that time I really was considering breaking my contract. Some of my conditions had not been met and I was very disappointed about the assistance I had received from official institutes. Moreover one should not forget that a considerable amount of money was being deducted from my salary to meet – oh, the irony of it – expenses for my accommodation; accommodation that I did not have. In retrospect I think that the good atmosphere in our family pulled us through. Fortunately, later on I was able to make a deal with the manager of the National Housing Corporation and he provided us with a house. It was September 1980 before we moved into a staff house, on the project. In all, over a period of one year we had changed houses three times. Apart from the inconvenience we found it very difficult to adjust to the new situations.

Giving a hand

One of the things one has to learn to live with is the regular requests for assistance, either privately or at the project. The requests vary from considerable amounts of money to jeans, which are very popular. Although we have not been unwilling to meet some of them, we have had to refuse more and more because the situation became untenable. Now we only consider requests from our own personnel, and even then there are limits. In the Netherlands we would exchange our childrens' clothing with other families when it became too small. Here we give it to our personnel or to some known labourers on the project. It is received so gratefully that we feel sorry that we did not take more used clothes along with us from home.

I should like to stress another aspect of giving assistance. That is the ease with which the labourers on the project expect that the project management will assist them in growing foodstuffs. I do not know whether this is because Tanzania receives much help from donors, which of course must be known by the common people, or that it is something incorporated in their way of life. I should like to grant a request to plough their lands and then let them do the rest of the work, but we now do the complete range of cultivation for them. In my opinion this is not a good thing. I do hope that they at least realize that they are privileged in comparison with their worse-off compatriots. I can, however, understand their feelings. It is hard to see all kinds of equipment that could make your daily work a lot easier standing about without being able to make use of it.

FROM PAPER TO PRACTICE

Without form and void

When we arrived in Tanzania, in October 1979, not only was our private accommodation not organized, the project could not be started because there was no land available. The Ministry of Agriculture was, however, going about purchasing a defunct sisal estate on which to establish the training centre. It was three months before the land was available. We were able to start developing the farms section by the first of February 1980, one of the conditions set by the identification missions. At that moment the Dutch team consisted of the farm manager and myself.

Unfortunately our efforts to lay out pastures and grow fodder crops partly failed, because of lack of rain. Moreover we did not have any machines. With a minimum of equipment we did succeed, however, in growing some sorghum, which was sold to a neighbouring farm. The training activities consisted of the surveying of the proposed site and the making of provisional plans and layouts for discussions with the architect and consulting engineer.

In November 1979, we placed orders for all machinery, including tractors, through what was then DTH. The orders were based on a list that had been discussed with a consulting institute in the Netherlands. Under normal conditions delivery of this farm machinery should have occurred in March or April 1980. Unfortunately nothing arrived, nor did we receive any confirmation about the order. Some time later, during a short visit to the Netherlands, I found that nothing had been done on this order. We reviewed the list again. Machines, tools and tractors started arriving in July 1980.

In June 1980 my team-mate, the farm manager, left Tanzania. His contract expired and he did not renew it for personal reasons. That meant that besides my other troubles I had to devote much time to the development and the activities of the farms section. The Tanzanian counterpart of the farm manager needed much guidance, although he was very interested and willing to assist.

For love or money

The two Tanzanian-Dutch identification and review missions had identified a wide range of possible candidates to be trained. Figures had been derived from the surveys of the Dairy Development Plan of Tanzania. However the amount of money allocated by the Government of the Netherlands was not enough to establish a training centre with the facilities required for training thirty-two trainees at a time. When I mentioned this at the Netherlands Embassy in Dar Es Salaam the reaction was that we should start first and indicate the amount of money still required. This money could be raised during following bilateral negotiations on the technical aid programme between Tanzania and the Netherlands. This approach was not acceptable to DGIS in The Hague. I had to stick to the allocated amount of money. However, the plans and provisional training programme I had made could not be realized within this budget.

44

While considering the training programme I found that a total intake of 40 trainees was more advisable than 32:
– thirty-two students is too many for theory lessons, but two groups of 16 trainees for theory lessons is uneconomic
– a group of 40 can be easily divided in two groups of 20, which also makes it possible to conduct simultaneously two courses different in level and duration
– two groups imply that the utilization of facilities like classroom and teaching aids and materials is high
– twenty students per group is a good number for theory lessons. When this group is divided into practical groups the number will never exceed eight. This was a pre-condition set by the first identification mission.

Consequently, I made my plans for the buildings and prepared calculations to fix the number of classrooms and other facilities. As there were no detailed plans and designs available, neither in Tanzania nor in the Netherlands, I relied very much on my experience in practical training, supported by some papers published by FAO.

In my plans I had already allowed for a possible increase in the number of trainees, which was foreseen by the first identification mission. On this issue the manual 'Farmer training in East, Central, and Southern Africa' reports:

> It is quite common for training centres to be built under a phased programme; Phase I may cater for 30 beds, and Phase II for an additional 30 beds. In such cases the hall and kitchen should be built to the ultimate planned capacity of the centre. Even outside phased programmes, kitchens and halls should be built in generous proportions, because training centres are nearly always extended in size over the years.

All my plans and designs had been approved by the Director of Manpower of the Ministry of Agriculture in Dar Es Salaam.

Being rapped over the knuckles

In the meantime DGIS had decided to add a construction supervisor to our team. Since this supervisor had instructions from DGIS to minimize capital investments regardless of the consequences, our discussions were not always friendly. I had no doubt about his technical expertise, but he clearly had no knowledge of practical training in dairy cattle husbandry. To accept those modifications and alterations in my plans and layouts would have meant a negative influence on the quality of the training, on the well-being of the trainees and of all staff. In my opinion a well-designed environment stimulates both trainees and staff.

A representative of DGIS arrived to help overcome the difficulties that had arisen by exceeding the allocated budget. A tender, which was already set in motion, was stopped, because the contractors' quotes for some reason were very high. Much to my regret the matter was tackled from a strictly formal point of view. To me it was not only a question of cost-benefit analysis. The quality of education and training cannot be expressed simply in terms of capital investments. The whole situation ended in a stalemate and I was requested to review my plans and present an alternative plan that did not exceed the allocated budget.

His Masters changing voice

Many of the things that went wrong may be partly blamed on reorganizations within the backstopping institutions in the Netherlands. A reorganization at the Ministry of Foreign Affairs at The Hague (DTH became DGIS) caused a reshuffle of staff. The project officers whom I had dealt with before my departure to Tanzania had been replaced by others who considered the implementation of a project from a slightly different point of view. As a result the order for tractors and machines was not honoured because certain information on the planning schedule was missing. Although I had my own schedule for Tanga, this did not meet their requirements for project planning.

My approach was a more practical one, because we were trying hard to implement a project under conditions that only exist in one in twenty-five less developed countries. These conditions hardly permit textbook planning.

Two reorganizations also took place in Dar Es Salaam, one at a critical point, directly after the Director of Manpower Development in the Ministry of Agriculture had approved the plans and designs for the project. Because of this time-consuming reorganization I was left sitting with these plans. In March 1980 the centre was shifted from the Ministry of Agriculture to the Ministry of Livestock Development and Natural Recourses, and to another division, viz. the Division of Livestock Production. As a result I had to establish new contacts and explain the purpose of the project again. After the parliamentary and presidential elections a new Ministry of Livestock Development was established. The training centre is now called a Livestock Training Institute (abbreviated LITI). Since this new Ministry is solely concerned with livestock production I believe this will be an advantage for the centre. The training centre now falls under the Director of Research and Training. Fortunately almost all staff who were acquainted with the training centre were reposted to this new Ministry. In this way this last reorganization had only minor effects.

The show must go on

By the end of 1980 I had drawn up a new Plan of Operations that contains the following features:
– the number of trainees will be forty, divided in two groups of twenty, which allows the training/programmes/courses to differ in duration and level of training
– the number of lactating cows has been reduced from 300 to 175. Apart from lactating cows there will also be the dry and pregnant cows, and heifers and calves. The cattle will be held on one large scale farm, one medium scale farm and three small scale farms, to present all available dairy farming systems in Tanzania.

I was forced to take drastic measures with the social component of the project

46

by reducing the staff housing. All but the housing for labourers has been removed from the list of the Dutch contribution. This has made the set-up more modest, but the capital investments were outstripping the total amount of money that had been allocated to the project by the Dutch government.

During discussions with representatives of the Ministry of Livestock Development, the Netherlands Embassy and DGIS, the Tanzanians accepted my new plan of operations with one amendment. The project implementation should be phased to start with twenty trainees. If this proved successful and the demand for this type of training is strong enough a second phase could be implemented that would increase the number of trainees to forty. The work done by the earlier identification missions has fallen victim to all these alterations and changes. Their suggestions and recommendations in some cases have been ignored or interpreted in a completely different way than they were first made. However my counterpart and I have been asked to readjust a major part of our plan of operations to match more closely the identification mission's original plan. I hope that will be the end of all the problems on how to establish and implement the training centre.

Now that the plan of operations is no longer an issue, are all our problems over? I am afraid there will always be new problems. That is simply inherent in the process of implementing a project. For instance, in the future I expect some difficulties with:
– the supply of construction materials
– the housing of Tanzanian staff of higher level, because the Ministry of Livestock Development is only able to raise limited funds
– the supply of materials from the Netherlands, because all orders must be supported by documents that clearly prove that they are necessary
– the acquisition of cattle in Tanzania, since it is extremely difficult to obtain good quality cattle
– the tuning of all activities in the plan of operations so that as few delays as possible occur for the lowest possible cost.

LAST BUT NOT LEAST

Ideals and reality

One of the reasons that I wanted to go to Tanzania was to contribute to the policy of self-reliance proclaimed by President Mwalimu Julius K. Nyerere. Although it is not a source of problems for me, my ideas about helping people have changed. In spite of the fact that the present policy has very many good aspects (rural health centres, primary education, water-pumps throughout the country, etc.), I sometimes have the impression that people lose interest in this ideal. A hard-working man can earn some money, but he will be heavily taxed, and there are few things to buy with the money that is over.

Many farmers who for years have been growing export crops now tend to concentrate on food crops, because the prices they receive from the production boards or crop authorities are too low to meet their production costs. Tanzania faces a shortage of foreign currency, which makes it difficult to buy necessary items like spare parts, fuel and oil. The decreasing production of export crops, such as coffee, will worsen the situation.

Nor are some of the production boards and crop authorities to which farmers are bound to sell their produce functioning as efficiently as they might. Sometimes they operate with too much formality and bureaucracy. A typical example is that of the labourers who went to town in the morning to collect concentrates from a parastatal, which has the monopoly to sell these concentrates. They returned without the concentrates because somebody said that they were not available. The day before, when the farm manager was there, he was told that the required concentrates were available in large quantities. This meant that five labourers and a tractor and trailer have been away for one morning, for nothing. You can't help get the impression that the people employed in some parastatals, crop authorities and production boards are not sufficiently interested in rendering service.

Whatever will be

Since we have not yet started a regular training programme I have not noticed any pressure from political sources. However, when we begin preparing curricula, syllabi and the lecture notes possibly we will have to choose programmes that will cut costs, which implies that less labourers will be employed. I am afraid this will cause some pressure from political sources to keep our labour force at present levels, even when this is not economically feasible.

Furthermore, it might be difficult to introduce some farm management techniques that could lead to better results. I think that, for example, it will not be possible to introduce cultivation of maize to make silage, for feeding it to the cattle. In this case we will certainly be reminded that maize is a staple food for the local population. This will not cause me problems, but I know that some Tanzanians do not agree because they see the advantages of feeding maize silage to cows instead of sorghum silage.

Because we are still in the preparatory phase of the project we have not had to cope with didactic problems. However, when I look for possible sources of problems I know they will surely come from there, too.

What can I do for you?

Taking into consideration my experiences, you might get the impression that development work in a developing country is nothing but a string of problems. Fortunately there are so many other factors that make a stay in a developing country really something enjoyable. The knowledge that one can do something for the local people who, in general, are interested in your activities, the tropical climate, the life-style to be enjoyed with wife and children, the possibility to observe other cultures and to visit places of interest, this all makes it worthwhile to experience. After all, I came to ask, 'What can I do for you?'

48

5   TRAVEL BY BUS

David and Hennie van der Schans

WORKING NEAR LAKE VICTORIA

We lived and worked for more than three years at the Ministry of Agriculture Training Institute Nyegezi, in Tanzania. The institute is situated in a training complex, with many different schools and institutes. The surroundings of the complex are fabulous: gentle sloping lands with occasional rock outcrops, towering like statues over the valleys. Further on the shores of Lake Victoria can be seen. Besides the agricultural institute, there are three secondary schools, a fisheries institute for research and training and a social training centre.

Most of these institutes were founded by the Roman Catholic Mission and gradually taken over by the Tanzanian government after independence. All the students, teachers and workers of the schools and institutes live at Nyegezi. Near Nyegezi, there are many small villages where the people still live in the traditional way.

The Nyegezi centre is a social enclave for the expatriates working there, although it is managed by Tanzanians with, mostly, a European education. There is electricity and running water. Buildings are constructed out of concrete bricks. This contrasts with the villages just outside the compound, behind the dormitories of our students. The way of life in the villages is as it has been for hundreds of years. Only the portable radio and the bicycle testify to the times in which we live.

There, at Nyegezi, we made a shy entry. We tried to forget where we came from and keep ourselves open to this new life. There are difficulties in the beginning due to cultural differences. We had to learn from the mistakes we made, but we found rest, patience, kindness and a tremendous hospitality. In the first place we had to learn how to behave. It is useless to stand on a pedestal and dictate. You have to investigate the existing situation and use that as a basis for contact.

A CULTURE SHOCK

When we finally departed for Tanzania six weeks of preparation to become a development worker lay behind us, but we were anxious to go and experience the life 'over there'. We were told how to survive the culture shock, how to be-

have and react to the local culture. About fifteen rather idealistic people, most of whom had just finished their studies, chose to become volunteers. It would be our first working experience. We had been already teaching biology and chemistry at a secondary school for domestic science in the Netherlands. Hennie is also qualified to teach horticulture. I (David) had signed the volunteer contract but we hoped that we would both get a job that would give us the opportunity to fight shoulder-to-shoulder with the Africans for the development of Tanzania. We were overwhelmed by solidarity with our fellow world-citizens.

Two weeks before we left, the last details of assignment arrived and we could now be sure that we were going to a training institute of the Ministry of Agriculture near Mwanza. It was not yet clear which duties we had to fulfil but, anyway, we had all our books with us and we were prepared to do anything required of us. Also, vague promises had been made about Hennie getting a job and a contract, so when we arrived we were very optimistic.

One day after our arrival in Tanzania we left on our first long journey by train: Dar es Salaam – Tabora in 24 hours. A train full of black people. Finally we were among them, our target group, Africans. Those who act so differently, are so little developed. We were tongue-tied; in spite of our Kiswahili course, we could not yet distinguish a word in the rattling chorus of the voices around us. At Tabora, where we stayed two weeks with another volunteer, at an agricultural institute, we learned a lot more about putting solidarity into practice. With World Bank funds, an Italian constructor was rebuilding the institute, because the students were being taught in old tobacco barns. The project, which cost more than a million US dollars provided for very luxurious school buildings and, especially, staff housing. Staff houses were built in three grades, A, B and C. An unmarried tutor with an university degree lives in a big, Grade A house; a labourer with a wife and children lives in a small two-room, Grade C house! These were the first things in contradiction with our feelings of solidarity. There was no equality. There were privileged people in Tanzania, too: those who could take more than their fair share. It is incorporated in the system of housing. Just like back home.

OUR NEW HOME

Shortly after this trip to Tabora, we went via Dar es Salaam to Mwanza, our final destination. For the second time we boarded the train, this time for a forty-hour journey. It is the longest train journey you can make in Tanzania. We already felt at home among Africans. We really felt great travelling in this way, particularly because there were only a few other Europeans on the train. The number of Europeans in a certain situation seemed to us to indicate our degree of integration in African life. On the last part of our journey we travelled together with one of Tanzania's most popular bands, the Tabora Jazz Band. They were invited to play at the agricultural school where we were going to work. This coincidence gave us a feeling of integration. As we write this we are aware that it sounds a bit overdone, but the will to integrate, to know and un-

51

derstand Africans, made each contact with parts of their life an experience.

The advertisement of the organization we worked for promised us 'work at the grass-roots level'. We had that idea in mind when we arrived. But soon we began to look upon this phrase very sarcasticly. During the first three months of our stay, for example, we lived in the biggest house of the compound. An expatriate expert and his family used to live in the house but they had gone on home-leave. So we looked after the house. And we could get used to having a houseboy, a shamba-boy (garden-boy) and a night-watchman. It was an excellent opportunity to practise Kiswahili. We talked almost every night with Raymund, Juma and Lyakurwa. But imagine living in a big house with servant quarters and three servants. That was really quite different from what we had expected. And we thought it was exceptional, but to our astonishment we noticed that almost all Europeans, volunteers like us included, lived in luxurious houses with large shambas (gardens), so that they also needed a houseboy, a shamba-boy and a night-watchman for safety. This luxurious life has become so normal among Europeans in the towns that they often claim the best houses in town areas, where the colonists used to live. You start doubting your mental make-up if a situation is in such contradiction with your ideas. But luckily there are a few people who refuse to conform to this way of life. They try hard to minimize the contrast between their way of life and that of the Tanzanian in a comparable situation.

It is always difficult to find the golden mean. This is often a personal matter. As we looked upon it, when we were at Nyegezi we should live among our colleagues in a normal way, in a brick house and not in a local house in the village. But we felt we should live in such a way that a number of African colleagues would not feel a barrier to come to our house and we should not feel shy to go to theirs. And we think we succeeded in doing that. Even now, a few years after returning to Europe, we still get letters from colleagues and we keep in touch with them. Nevertheless there are many things in the African way of life that we do not understand or experience in the way our Tanzanian friends understand and feel them.

JUMA'S PLACE

We came to experience each visit to a village, a conversation with a farmer or an invitation to visit someone's house as a privilege. After three years we still had the feeling of surprise and of being honoured when we were invited to visit. Some of those who invited us did so to show their compatriots that they had good relations with a *mzungu* ('white man').

This was not the case when Juma, the houseboy of an European colleague, invited us to his house to introduce us to his wife. He had gone to his home area and married a woman from his village whom his parents had chosen for him. She had come with him from Morogoro to Mwanza, a distance of a thousand kilometres. As he was a servant they lived in a two-room Grade C house. When we arrived that Sunday afternoon we were installed in the living-room. Juma remained with us but his wife immediately started working. She offered us a glass of lemonade and began preparing the food. In the same room where we were sitting she washed the rice, extracted milk from a coconut and went outside to cook it as it was done in her home area. In the meantime the conversation with Juma continued, but his wife did not participate at all. Then the food was served, but again she ate separately, with her sister. The rice with coconut extract and chicken was delicious. After the meal it was time to depart and Juma and his wife accompanied us. It is a custom that the guests are accompanied on their way home. During this walk we were able to have a short conversation with Juma's wife.

VILLAGE LIFE

Of course I (David) had other contact with life in the villages. One day Sina, one of my colleagues, came to me and asked me to go with him to a medicine man about sixty kilometres away. His cousin was mentally disturbed. She was singing hymns and murmuring phrases the whole day long, and there was a vacant look in her eyes. I had been in Tanzania for three years, but this was to be the first time I was to see a medicine man practising his profession. To my African colleagues a *mganga* ('medicine man') is nothing special, however. As the writer of 'African religions and philosophy' John Mbiti (London, 1969) said:
> 'Every village in Africa has a medicine man within reach, and he is the friend of the community. He is accessible to everybody at almost all times, and comes into the picture at many points in individual and community life'.
> 'Their personal qualities vary but they are expected to be trustworthy, upright morally, friendly, willing and ready to serve, able to discern peoples needs and not be exorbitant in their charges'.

The mganga talked with us. He would take Sina's cousin in. He had more patients. Sina got a list of herbs he had to buy at the market. These herbs were his cousin's medicines. After three weeks we went again to see his cousin, who was improving. She worked in the mganga's fields and acted more normal. But still she had to remain there, and Sina got a new list of herbs and a bill. Later I heard she had been cured and that she was living with her family again.

THE JOB

We went to Tanzania with expectations that were completely different from those we would have had at home. We became development workers because we thought we could help in the development of Tanzania. When we started we looked at the situation very critically. Looking critically you find more imperfections than an ordinary spectator. We regarded every practice that was in contradiction with our ideas about education, agriculture or life-style distrustfully. We were not very critical of practices that conformed with our habits and ideas. Of course everybody is like this, but it does hamper an objective comparison.

Especially during the first few months at Nyegezi, we were confronted with so many new impressions that an evaluation was hardly possible. We lived every new experience intensely and reacted to the new situation in our own way. We were in a labyrinth, trying to find our way without having a map to guide us to the end of it.

When we arrived at Nyegezi the students had just gone on holidays, so we had an excellent opportunity to acclimatize.

> During one of the first weeks I (David) was in the principal's office when a telephone call came from the neighbouring institute. They asked for somebody to do a topographical and soil survey of their farm so they could implement a better system of land management. I was nominated to do the job with the assistance of three graduates of the centre. The area was badly managed, soil fertility was very low and erosion rills crossed the fields. Theoretically it was possible to improve the field but it would cost a lot of money and, above all, it would need good management. I planned the work to take three weeks. I developed a plan to improve the area and did the survey. But after one week, two of my assistants appeared to have lost their motivation, and none of them really understood what we were doing. Although they were graduates from the land-use planning course, they were not up to the job. All the things they had been taught, they had just copied but not understood. There was not sufficient time to finish the project and my suggestions – simple soil conservation measures – were not accepted by the principal of the institute. He had already discussed the matter and felt that there should be a plan for large-scale terracing, which nobody had ever done before or even seen practised.

Now, a few years after all this happened, I can think quietly about it and put all the events and the persons into perspective and evaluate the things that happened. But when I was doing the survey I worked under pressure to finish the job in time. I had expectations of the people I worked with and I had certain ideas about how to solve the problem technically. Here was a European thinking too much in a European way.

After about six months, a directive from the ministry came to prepare an improved land-use planning course. The present course did not deliver competent workers. The course should have as objective to teach the students to plan villages. Together with some Tanzanian colleagues, we translated this into a syllabus. The students would work in the villages and plan the area so that every piece of land would be used according to its capacity for economic production. This would involve surveys, planning and execution of the plans, selection of suitable crops, measures to protect the land against depletion, and measures to enable a more intensive form of agriculture.

Over ninety percent of the Tanzanian population lives from agriculture. The only way to improve the situation of the Tanzanian rural population is to improve their possibilities of production.

My task was then clear. The first months had been rather aimless. The teaching was aimed at a very low level and there were many other teachers who could teach my subjects at that level. The fact that most of my colleagues did not teach more than seven periods per week did not contribute to my motivation. However this new task, to set up a new style of land-use planning course, made the rest of my stay at Nyegezi very pleasant and effective.

Still, I used to teach more than my Tanzanian colleagues. I had quite some problems with the class size and number of students per practical group. But for my colleagues it was no problem to teach seventy students at the same time or to have a practical group of thirty-five students. In my struggle for smaller classes and a more practical approach of teaching I failed. During meetings, my colleagues would admit that it is better to teach small groups. But it could never be realized in the timetable.

BASIC EDUCATION

Development implies education, but education does not necessarily bring about development. Many of my students aimed at getting a white-collar job through the course. They looked upon their study as a means to make life easier and to get higher status with a minimum of effort.

But the policy of the Tanzanian Government is based on extension work in the villages. Village life is tough, and of all the possible technical solutions to problems only very few are feasible. The expatriate experts usually teach and their students are supposed to go into the villages. What knowledge is useful to these students? Very little of what is being taught at the training institute originates from Tanzania. A selection should be made of practices applicable under Tanzanian conditions. The expatriate is expected to do this without having hardly any idea about these specific conditions.

> The first year I taught my students a great number of periods on terracing. Terracing is very labour-intensive unless it is practised on highly mechanized large-scale farms. But neither labour nor machinery are available in Tanzania. Other systems of land management which can easily be practised in villages need more emphasis. After having seen life in villages I could adjust my course and give some examples of practicable solutions. From these the students got some useful ideas about implementing terracing in the villages.

The course program comprised fifty percent theory classes and fifty percent practicals. So there is far more emphasis on practicals than at the agricultural schools in the Netherlands. I was very pleased when I heard this. But I found out later that the students are kept busy during practicals with very small tasks and the theory teachers do not know how to transfer their knowledge into practicals. Knowledge is so often regarded literally as a source of income in itself. Almost all my colleagues had never practised the things they were teaching. Their study programmes aimed to give them a theoretical background as quickly as possible and then they were left to their own resources to teach these theoretical issues to others. Only very inventive students develop a critical attitude and do something with their knowledge. But the inventive people are the ones that start private farms or are offered high salaries by companies. Government institutions are not the first places where you find the 'motors' of development. It is important to realize these facts before judging the situation.

The lack of creativity and motivation of ones colleagues is very irritating. The civil servant mentality of drawing a salary for lowest possible input cannot be excused and should be opposed as strongly as possible. (Nevertheless we should try to realize what the situation would be like back home with no salary increase for ten years and over 400 percent inflation during that period).

A course that provides only technical skills or background knowledge is inadequate. Theory and practice are like sand and stones: they will only make a building when used in the proper combination. The actual process of building is development. We should know what to do with our technical knowledge so that it will be suitable for further development. Moreover we should know about the building's foundation before we can work on further technical development of any Third World country.

BEING A STUDENT

Most institutes for further education, such as secondary, technical and agricultural schools, are boarding-schools. To live in a boarding-school means that you always are close to your work. The people you work with are the same people you meet socially. We experienced this in the agricultural school, where the students were adults, and in the secondary school.

In the secondary school the whole day is neatly organized for the pupils. They are controlled twenty-four hours a day. They have to ask permission for each and everything. The early morning parade, especially, is quite a happening. Classes are lined up every morning in ranks. The headmaster, headmistress or teacher on duty inspects the students: finger nails clean, shoes polished, no missing buttons, ears washed, hair combed, etc. Every student who is not perfectly dressed and washed gets some punishment, given by the teacher on duty. Every teacher has his share of duty; I had it too. Walking through the rows of waiting students, inspecting them, made me feel uncomfortable.

And then there is the matter of corporal punishment. The first time I (David) saw this, I couldn't believe my eyes. There was a girl on her hands and knees on the floor being beaten on her buttocks with a stick because she took her letter from the teacher's desk before the teacher had read it. I have seen a group of students passing through the corridor on their knees with their chairs above their heads, because they were too noisy. Such punishment did not happen often. In some schools, working in the fields was considered to be a punishment.

In the secondary school both teachers and students make long days. The children are kept busy the whole day and in the spare moments they play sport or laze about. In the agricultural institute the students were much older and they were free to do in their spare time whatever they liked. All sorts of sporting clubs and a photo club are organized after classes. Sports tutors are nominated

56

to organize the sports events, e.g. soccer, basketball or volleyball matches. But all these events have to be held after classes, which start at eight in the morning and end at five o'clock in the afternoon. So most of the students prefer to drink a soft drink or just sit in the shade and talk. The students take their meals in the dining hall. They all have their own plate and mug, which they wash after dinner. When the food is not good, as on one particular sunday, when the meat had gone bad, they know where to find the person in charge, usually a female teacher in food science.

THE FEMALE TUTOR

One-quarter of the teachers at the agricultural institute were women. They taught various subjects, such as horticulture, extension, soil science, nutrition and animal husbandry. For the first six months of our stay, I (Hennie) worked with a Tanzanian colleague. We taught horticulture. There were very few girls on the course but then agriculture is not a favourite subject for girls to study. The principal had the opinion that women would not be very useful because they would get married, have children and would therefore not be able to participate in the ministries or other jobs in administration or management. Although married female tutors functioned normally at our institute, the principal still tried to get rid of female students. He almost succeeded when a part of our course had to be moved to another institute because it had to be expanded. He selected that part of the course that had most female students.

There was an American sister working in the livestock department. She was respected by both students and her colleagues and she managed to run the whole livestock section of the farm. She collected waste of grain mills for the piggery, poultry and dairy farm when there was no money to purchase concentrates. The livestock department was flourishing when she left. The work was continued by her Tanzanian colleagues. In general a female tutor was nothing special and she was accepted as a colleague or teacher. But when a woman made a mistake, it was ascribed to her being a woman.

WOMEN SHOULD NOT WHISTLE

There are many occasions when the position of a woman in African society becomes clear. Situations that do not seem strange to us, can be very strange to Africans. When we visited Juma, who is a Moslem, his wife had the role of serving the man and the guests. This was not in all families as strong as in Juma's case. Usually when we visited a colleague his wife remained with us and participated in the discussions – a daughter, cousin or servant prepared the food. When Tanzanians visited us they were amazed to see me sitting and talking while David prepared food, tea or coffee. To them, a man should not work in the kitchen.

It is also a married woman's duty to give her husband children. So when people heard that we were married they asked immediately how many children I had. When I said: 'I have no children', I often got the advice to give David some children, because that's what he 'expects of me'. Children are your insurance; they will look after you when you are old.

One day I was walking with a colleague to the garden when I saw David far away. I wanted to ask him something so I whistled through my fingers. Lyimo, my colleague, was astonished. 'You should not do this – whistle for attention – and certainly not a woman to a man'.

In the policy of the Tanzanian government the position of the woman is clearly described. The importance of the position of the woman in society is often emphasized. In President Nyerere's speeches he often accuses men of being lazy and exploiting women. Because of this policy many women have important positions in the villages and the UWT, the national women's organisation, is active in its struggle for an equal role for women in Tanzanian development.

TRAVEL BY BUS AND HAVE A BREAK-DOWN

Upon arriving in a country with a different culture and a different standard of living, everybody will meet problems. You have to adjust your ideas and life-style to new and then unknown attitudes. The way you will react to the differences depends on the way you judge the situation. We did it in our way and everybody will do it in theirs. Many Europeans lose their patience in the first month of their stay because they want to create organizations like the ones they are familiar with at home. As soon as they perceive their failure everything is blamed on 'these stupid Africans who cannot organize at all'. Other development workers judge the situation according to what is available in the shops. If cheese, butter, chocolate, beer and motorbikes are available then the supply system is good and the government has a good policy concerning transport and imports. But how many of the ninety percent of the rural population benefit from these commodities? Most Europeans make their acquaintance with a country in a town, where they can lead a rather 'European' life. We do not have to enter a local restaurant in the suburbs to fill our stomach with a simple dish for six Tanzanian shillings.

The stories told by Europeans who have been in the country for some time will have a great influence on your attitude towards 'normal' Tanzanian life. Many development workers are members of the elite clubs and make their social contacts at parties or through club members. But they seldom ask a Tanzanian colleague for explanations or to be introduced into their life.

Travel by bus and have a break-down. It may not be a very pleasant situation with one hundred passengers in a sixty-passenger bus, but you can see how people deal with difficulties. How they tolerate and make the best of it. Maybe when your bus has a break-down and you are sitting in the dust in the middle of nowhere you will wish you are in that car full of Europeans passing by at high speed. But you are not alone, you are there to work with your fellow passengers and you can only be effective when you understand their conditions.

58

6 COPPER BELT BLUES

Jan Willem Bulthuis

A FARM COLLEGE IN A MINING REGION

Kalulushi Farm College (KFC) lies under the smoke of the copper industry in the mining town of Kitwe. In this town, copper mining has reached its climax. Copper is the fountain of life in Zambia. The college was founded in the sixties by the World Council of Churches. Since then it has gone through several crises. In the seventies the college operated under the responsibility of a board of governors of the council. This board is no longer responsible to the World Council of Churches but to the Ministry of Agriculture and Water Development. Each year the ministry makes the college a grant, enough to cover the cost of the salaries. At this moment plans are ready for the ministry to take over the college completely. It will be absorbed into the government educational structure.

The aim of the KFC training programme is to prepare Zambians to go 'back to the land', to raise agricultural production. After they have finished this college the graduates are to start their own farm. Besides subsistance farming, there is only a small number of farmers producing cash crops. Because the copper industry has attracted many men away from the farms there is a shortage of food suppliers in the country, which has forced the government to import most of the food, consuming the benefits of the copper industry. Training people for farming is therefore a first priority that is strongly supported by the government. Despite this training only a few graduates of the college go into farming; the others prefer to be employed in other ways.

The college has an intake of forty to fifty students per year for a two year course. For various reasons only half of the college capacity is being used at present. The course includes animal husbandry (e.g. beef production, dairying and pig and poultry farming) and crop production (including rainfed crops, horticulture and growing of citrus fruits). Furthermore, a farm machinery course and a course on simple building are given. Theory and practicals are given in all subjects except English, biology, soil science and farm accounting, which are only taught in theory. During the ten-hour day, students spend thirty percent of their time in the classroom and the rest in the various production units.

Staff members live on the college premises, as well as the students, who live in the boarding-house. Compared to their homes – in the bush – the students

live in luxurious conditions in the boarding-house. Still their life at the college is not at all easy. They work hard and compared to Western standards their meals are sober, their clothing poor and they have little money to spend on essential commodities. Yet improvement of the standard of living of the students here could mean a great set-back when they actually have to go 'back to the land'. There they would not find electricity, a constant food supply, piped water and good housing. This set-back sometimes causes discouragement.

To me the usefulness of my working at the college is closely connected with the number of students actually going into productive farming on their own farm. I am not too optimistic about this and knowing the students opinion about the idea I have my doubts about training people to be farmers as we do at KFC. It is my opinion that KFC needs radical changes in staffing, entry qualifications and settling policy, changes requiring the ministry's co-operation.

ABOUT FRIENDS AND OTHERS

Generally speaking I have not come to grief with the people at the college, though there are exceptions. Privately, I only have contact with some of the other teachers and students. When I came to Zambia I did not expect to integrate deeply into Zambian society within the two years of my contract. There are many possibilities in and around Kitwe and throughout the country to make contacts. Therefore I do not feel obliged to look for many friends at the college and I have not felt it as a problem that I am not integrated in the college society. For the Zambians, however, who often see me alone in or around my house, I am a source of anxiety. Some students have told me that they do not regard it as normal to be alone or single at my age (26 years).

When I arrived here one of the teachers was acting-director of the college. The college was in a bad way and he had applied for six volunteers, four of which were supplied by ONV (Organisation of Netherlands Volunteers, SNV). These volunteers, three teachers and one accountant, were quite willing to assist in building up the college. However it became gradually obvious that the acting-director wanted to build up the college around his own person, for his personal interest. The volunteers advised the college's board of governors not to accept his application for the directorship. This advice was followed by the board and someone else became director. This Zambian is very willing to accept advice and to co-operate but for some reason sometimes he does not implement his decisions. There may be several reasons for this. Perhaps the director wants to avoid disappointing the expatriate: it is not considered polite to reject ideas or to refuse things on the spot. Besides, the director respects and sometimes even fears the power of the board of governors.

My relations with colleagues mainly depend on the individuals concerned. I tend to judge them according to what they are willing to do for the college. Some lecturers only have four hours of teaching per week, which is all they do for KFC. Students do notice the difference between qualified and willing members of staff and those who are not. This weakens the position of those who are not

61

doing much for the college, for which they compensate, or at least try to, by unpleasantnesses such as gossiping, sowing discord and bringing pressure to bear upon students in several ways. This does not, of course, have any positive effect on my relations with these lecturers.

I do not have many relations with the regional and local authorities. The existing contacts are not too bad, though I cannot get used to the habit of officials using their position to gain private privileges, such as the use of an official car – or worse. If a government official tries to use his power with me for private business, which luckily does not occur too much, I tend to give him a sound trouncing. Sometimes this causes problems later on if I have to deal with him on official business.

Problems with other volunteers at the college have risen from differences in opinion about the future development of the college. This issue, together with differences in character, has brought some tensions. By avoiding the controversial subjects and accepting the course of events, the misunderstandings have been reduced, but the basic differences of opinion have never been settled. Differences of opinion about our relations with Zambian colleagues have also been a source of disagreement. Relations among the volunteers have not been bad as such, but because you need each other more here, better relations would have been beneficial.

The relationships with family and friends at home have been very good though not intensive enough. My absence led to my girl-friend deciding to let our relationship cool down and later to her stopping it altogether, which is unpleasant. This type of event seems to occur more often. It is not difficult to understand but very difficult to accept. Because communications are poor, I sometimes feel quite helpless.

A WEALTHY STRANGER

For an ONV(SNV) volunteer, material problems cannot easily arise because of bad financial conditions. The only unpleasant thing I came across was the long period I had to wait before I could settle into my own house. It took almost one year before I could live on my own. During that time I had to move four times. Now I have a very nice house.

Sometimes I have the feeling that labourers and local staff take a wry look at me. My living allowance is twice as much as the earnings of a local staff-member with six children. Consequently there is quite a difference in possible living standards, which I think most of all shows in me having my own car. I have not faced any real problems with the differences as yet. People sometimes ask me for assistance in form of a loan, and I give according to the person and his needs. If I have the slightest suspicion that the money will be used for beer I do not assist, because it only generates more problems for the man and his family. Abuse of alcohol is a big problem in Zambia.

Because I do get a good living allowance, and because I have left my country for only a few years, Zambians automatically think that I came to earn a lot of money. Once they have accepted that I had other reasons for coming they cannot imagine that I am here voluntarily. Of course it is quite suspect if someone leaves his country for a short time to go to a country totally strange to him only to help strangers. What would you think if someone from the other side of the world came to live in your street to . . .?

FROM HAND TO MOUTH

Since its foundation the college has experienced several crises. One of the latest disasters was discovered in 1978, when the financial problems of the college were investigated. By practising fraud the previous director and accountant had enriched themselves, leaving the college with enormous debts when they were discharged. During my period of preparation in the Netherlands I was told that the financial situation as well as the organisation of KFC was rather bad. At that time I did not have the slightest idea what that could mean.

When I first arrived I did not see all the problems and complications. The situation did not look that bad to me. But the longer I was around the more I began to distinguish problems in staffing, finance, relationships, etc. The debts are almost cleared now, thanks to revenues from the well organized production unit and an additional government grant. But the struggle to meet the debts has affected the availability of funds within the college. Only the most urgent investments and repairs have been made, and only the most essential commodities have been bought for training purposes. Extensive handouts of notes and texts, and excursions and demonstration trials seem a bit too luxurious in this situation. Because of this chronic shortage of money, short-term planning is practised instead of sound budgeting. Only the clearance of debts, necessitated by threatened court action, can justify the financial shortcomings of training, however.

As I have said, the money to keep the college running has to come from the college production unit, supplemented by an annual government grant. In the near future, the government will take over the college. We are hoping, therefore, that more money will become available, but from what I know of the present financial position of government-financed institutions, this is rather doubtful. This can be no surprise when you consider the present financial state of Zambia and other countries in similar circumstances.

MONEY OR MANAGEMENT

The college is directed by a board of governors. This board has the authority to make the policy of the college. The motives of the board are not so clear to me, but what is very clear, however, is that the training of as many people as possible to become good farmers is not its first priority. Many of its decisions are contradictory, resulting in an inconsistant policy. This causes many problems in the day to day management of the college, especially because the board inter-

63

feres more in the daily running of the college than the staff likes. The college has two big handicaps: staffing and a money shortage. The first issue could be improved by the board of governors, via the director, but it seems that this is something it does not want to get involved in. Of seven teaching staffmembers, only two (including me) are qualified. Several of the teachers and instructors are KFC graduates but have had no extra training; the qualifications of the others are hardly any better. The college is overstaffed to a great extent (7 teachers plus instructors for 40 students) yet the board has never taken action to sack anybody, even if there is a clear reason. However, the college is legally influenced by external structures that affect staffing. It is hardly possible to dismiss an employee unless he has committed an obvious crime. This makes it difficult to get rid of unqualified, lazy and unco-operative people. The only two people who have been told to leave the college have been volunteers. Teachers are not replaced even when qualified Zambians are available. There are only requests for more volunteers.

Intakes of new students have been far below the school's capacity, to reduce total expenditures: more students need more food and other essential commodities. That extra production produced by more students would be more than the extra expenditure is a point that I cannot make understood. In view of these economic problems it is doubly difficult for me to understand why board members claim expenses for excellent meals, sitting allowances, and transport money for every meeting they attend. These expenditures equal the amount needed to accommodate all students for more than a fortnight. The board of governors is composed of a tribal chief, who holds rather important posts in the country, a council accountant, several farmers with good farms, a principal of another training institute, a provincial agricultural officer and a ministry official. It is possible that these people are, because of their quite responsible posts, not interested in the advice given by staff members, the director or the volunteers. Individually they are willing to discuss and to accept advice or to agree with one's opinion, but it is different when they are at a meeting.

In the beginning I had to get used to the differences in ideas about responsibility and delegation. Responsibility is only given in name and thus delegation is not really practised.

> I was put in charge of the garden production unit. In my Western view that meant that I was responsible for that unit and in fact director of that part of KFC. If I needed advice I could ask the director. In this case, however, I had to follow the detailed instructions he gave me about the day to day running of the garden. He instructed the workers and students himself, neglecting me, or he gave me instructions different from those he gave to the workers. Though we discussed the matter and he agreed with me about my concept of responsibility and delegation, his behaviour did not change.

A year after my arrival a new director was appointed. He had the intention of giving everybody a chance to do his part in improving the college. So a lot of committees were founded and a different organizational structure for the college administration was announced. Despite these fine intentions nothing has been put into practice, so that most of the committees are doing nothing.

The new director's indifference in the matter has weakened his position here.

Since the World Council of Churches pulled out, the college has not belonged to any other structure, but a take-over by the Zambian government will change this. No one, anywhere, knows what changes this will bring, even though the take-over could occur next week. Nor has preparation for the change in management been very good so far. This college will be the first one of its kind within the Ministry of Agriculture and Water Development, so there is no example that can serve as a model.

FROM WHENCE COMETH OUR SALVATION?

Politics is a sensitive issue in Zambia, and I must be very careful what I say about it. I must realize that I am a stranger. Yet strangers have their opinions. The political system in this country is different from ours in Western Europe. Zambia, like many African countries, is ruled by one party. Party members are to be found in all sectors and institutions of society, including our college society. Discussion with these persons is possible but they are very sensitive about criticism of the party. A few times I have even been told to mind my words. This is difficult when you come from a country where there is complete freedom of speech.

Practically speaking UNIP (United National Independence Party) wields the legislative, executive and judicial power. I cannot get accustomed to the misuse of that power by officials in private lives, practising favouratism and helping themselves as they do.

Since independence, the country has had to cope with many problems. In particular there is a desperate need for human resources. I doubt whether all Zambians are in favour of UNIP but those who criticize the official policy still find it difficult to organize themselves in such a way that they can express their feelings. Criticism becomes particularly acute when it concerns the 'all talk but no action' record of UNIP. Politicians often make tours throughout the country. Citizens are supposed to welcome them. KFC is near to the airport of Kitwe and therefore the college is often closed for a day to allow teachers and students to practise the ritual of meeting an important politician.

ONV does not allow its volunteers to be politically active, which has probably protected me from a lot of trouble. Still I think that it is only fair to mention these kinds of personal frustrations in this account. Sparing the rod in this respect would not only mean spoiling the child but also myself.

A STRANGER IN JERUSALEM

When I came to Africa I certainly intended to accept other ways of behaviour of the people I had to work with. Some time after my arrival, however, though the intention was still there, I found it hard to put that resolution into practice. Language is a source of problems. First there is the problem of two people not

65

using and understanding each others language. Speaking English to a woman who only knows Bemba (vernacular) will not lead to misunderstanding, but there will not be any understanding either. Second there are the difficulties of two people using the same language, but not being able to understand each other because they do not feel or interpret it similarly.

As the official language, English is used in class-room teaching. Outside classes, however, the Zambians talk among themselves in the vernacular. A student's ability in English is one of the points on which they are selected for the course. Even so, sometimes confusion and misunderstandings between the Zambians and me do occur. A well known example of this is the use of terms of abuse. Mostly, we Westerners do not pay much attention to those terms, but a Zambian will take the words literally; he will feel shocked and even offended. But there are many more sources of misunderstanding.

> I let myself in for some trouble with the students when I compared their system of digestion, in a carelessly chosen example, with that of a pig. They took that literally and they thought that I was comparing them with pigs. During the following discussion they even went as far as to conclude that they were pigs. I was accused of colonialism, racism and whatever other words fit into the jargon of that diatribe.

Discussion of examples used to explain an idea or a subject often leads to digression. At the same time the actual point of discussion falls into the background. In class I often notice that examples are remembered quite well but the actual subject is not even recognized.

In my dealings with Zambians I have not yet become used to what I will call equivocating. Straightforward answers and straightforward opinions are rare. To me this is a source of misunderstanding and also a source of anger. Many times agreements are not met, causing much inefficiency.

I think it is necessary to say a few words about witchcraft. Witchcraft is associated with events that cannot be clarified intellectually but still call for some explanation. The less one can explain the more the reason for happenings to be ascribed to witchcraft. Even people who I would describe as quite sensible refer to it in their stories. One thing is clear to me: most Zambians do believe in witchcraft in one way or the other, even in the Copperbelt, where many people have adopted a more or less Western style of life. Initially I thought that church-going people did not believe in witchcraft, but I am not so certain about that anymore. Several students have left the college, temporarily or for good, because they thought themselves to be bewitched. Even the director had the idea that he had been subjected to witchcraft during the first weeks of his stay here. Personally I have never experienced anything that I can put down to witchcraft, but I do not ridicule it as I did in the beginning, partly not to offend the Zambians.

THEIR LAW AND MY ORDER

Especially in the first months of my stay I made a lot of comparisons with the way things were at home. In the legal system I discovered quite a few differences, the traditional as well the 'modern' system. I have the impression that here, more than in the Netherlands, power is derived from money. Position in society or politics interferes with justice. Fraudulent behaviour – a crime of the privileged – is not always punished, but a poor boy stealing some oranges from the yard will be jailed for several months. I would not say that bribing is the cause of this type of justice. But it is said that a good lawyer, demanding a high payment, can get acquittal even in cases of obvious guilt. This may be the reason why some wealthy persons don't seem to be afraid of becoming involved in obscure practices, because their power will get them off the hook. It is of course possible that back home these practices are much better kept secrets.

Among Zambians, there is a feeling of inequality that originates from differences in power and position. But their tribe of origin is also very important. Several times at the college students have come to me to complain about a member of staff marking or treating them differently because of their tribe. In this respect it is an advantage to be an expatriate. The Zambians cannot accuse you of tribalism or favouratism.

Differences also show regarding the sense of justice. The truth for a Zambian can sound to me as a lie. Borrowed money is hardly ever returned, unless the creditor can show that he really is in need of his property. Sometimes I even wonder whether a feeling of guilt, which I would have if I owed someone something I had not returned, is present in most Zambians. If a Zambian wants to have something I have, he expects me to give it to him, especially if I have it in abundance. To him it is unfair if I do not give him something that I possess. In general, private ownership does not seem to have the same meaning here as in Europe. These are just some of the differences that create conflict between the traditional and 'modern' legal system, which is based on British law. The people do not think British, of course.

ME AND THE OTHERS

In few places in society are there equal rights for men and women. Mostly, however, the woman is all but the family slave, though the children also get quite a bit to do. In my view the woman has many duties and very few rights. Families are big, which causes difficulties with nutrition, hard labour for the mother, and problems with education and housing, etc. Mothers do many things that could also be done by their husbands, but they hardly pay attention if women complain about their situation. My observations may not be applicable, however, to traditional Zambian society as found in remote areas; the Copperbelt is urban.

When I first began at the college it surprised me that students or workers were very submissive when they came to ask me a question or a favour. Some went as far as kneeling when they spoke to me. I told them that they could come to me as to anybody else. Students were in the habit of standing up when they wanted to raise a question or give an answer. In doing so they had to move their chair with metal legs backwards on the concrete floor, causing enough noise to wake the dead. Moreover it took much time. I told them to remain seated, which was very difficult for them to accept, probably because they were used to the custom from childhood. Later on I was criticized by Zambian colleagues because, they argued, doing it my way the students showed less respect. Respect, shown by this type of behaviour, is an essential virtue in the eyes of Zambian teachers. Because I cannot accept that respect depends on this type of humility, the students in my classes remain seated. Other signs of respect shown towards Zambian colleagues are laughing even if a 'joke' is not funny, and not arguing much with a lecturer to avoid embarrassing him. To me it does not look genuine, though it might be.

Students and staff often describe the relations between these two groups in father-child terms. The director, for example, is referred to as the village headman. If it was only a matter of giving names I would not object, but the meaning is taken literally. Some students are ten years or more older than me, yet they regard teachers, including me, as real fathers. This may be a traditional attitude but to me it is very difficult to accept this comparison and I have told my students so. I very much like to help them with their problems as far as their study and their future as a farmer is concerned but personal problems of all kinds are not in my line. To me they are adults and they should be able to look after themselves. Besides, I believe that people of such different cultures need help from people of their own culture in solving their personal problems. In my opinion students who within two years are expected to be able to take care of themselves, should indeed be able to stand on their own now. Otherwise it will be extremely hard for them to become independent farmers after graduating.

THE SACRED SYSTEM OF SCHOOLING

In Zambia great efforts are made to educate as many people as possible, so there are very many primary and secondary schools spread throughout the country. There is, however, a lack of good teachers, especially in the remote areas. People are reluctant to go so far away into 'the bush' to teach. Classes are big and money for equipment is scarce. Because of this, as I discovered later on during my stay here, the level of primary school leavers (Grade 7) and of many secondary school leavers (Form I, II and III) is not what it should be. Not only is the general level low, but there are special problems with subjects like arithmetic and general science, which are fundamental for the subjects I teach. Moreover many of the Form III pupils and those with lower qualifications have problems in understanding the English language.

In the first half of secondary school, nobody can stay down; all move from Form I through to Form III, at which stage they sit for a nation-wide examination. A Form III failure can therefore be no better than a good Grade 7 leaver. There is a remarkable difference between Form III pupils that have failed and passed. Form IV and V graduates have the basic knowledge I should like all my students to have.

The schools use competition often as an incentive to stimulate their pupils to do better. Competition seems to play a role in the college too. This could be seen when we took two classes in which good and less good students were mixed and split them into one class of good students and one of less good students. The selection was based on the results of the previous term. This was done for the benefit of both groups and to make teaching easier. The students protested heavily. They argued that they had never experienced anything like it. The less good students felt really inferior to the other group, and began calling themselves 'the dull'. Now, half a year later, they are beginning to see the benefits of the separation: there is more individual attention and their level of understanding is better. The group of better students likes the idea also, because lessons are made more interesting for them. However if it was up to the students, they would choose to mix up the classes again.

THE HAPPY FEW

A student who wishes to enter the college must have proper qualifications and show genuine motivation. The difference in educational level is very great within the present group, which causes problems within classes. Some students are not very quick in understanding, but they do not dare interrupt or raise a question. If one of them does ask for an explanation, delaying the others, he is told (in Bemba) by the rest of the class to stop asking questions. Then there are the better ones. They ask relevant questions and demand explanations that will, however, never be grasped by the ones that are slow in understanding. In some cases I ask the better students to explain to the slow ones in private, since relations among the students are very good. In other cases I invite the slower learners to my house.

Because of the great differences between the students in the present group, the minimum requirement for entry to the college has been changed from Grade 7 to Form II. However level of education is not the most important criterion of selection. Proper motivation is of more importance for entrance as a student. The majority of the applicants seem to be aware of this requirement. When asked about their motivation, most students answer, 'I like to learn by doing, so that after graduation I can start my own farm'. Out of the previous group of graduates three are known to be farmers. Nothing is known of the other 37 graduates. At this moment, three months before graduation, 20 per cent of the present group are trying to get a piece of land and a loan. The others do not seem to be interested in starting a farm, while at the start of the course all of them expressed the wish to become farmers. They now want to start working somewhere as an employee. Though they are not suitable for the position most of them hope to become a farm manager. Becoming a farm-hand or a commodity demonstrator are the alternatives, but the training they get here is not suitable for these jobs.

There are other motivations for joining the college. Entering the college means for most of the present students that after finishing their pre-education they can continue studying straight away, and that really is something in Zambia. First of all because chances to carry on studying are few. Second it postpones the moment upon which they have to take care of themselves, and that is very important in a country where the rate of unemployment is very high. The college provides them with shelter and they may even learn useful things. Students are relieved from the responsibility they must meet in the outside world; they are looked after by the college. The college provides them with food and even some pocket money. Moreover they can have a good time with friends. It will be very hard to improve selection. In my view it is necessary, though, because KFC is no charitable institution.

Perhaps it would be wiser to recruit a different type of student? Older and thus more mature students are presumably more independent and more determined. The applicant should also have a little capital to start with. Then you automatically get a group of people that has been working for a few years, that also has some self discipline. At the moment there are only a few of this kind of trainee at KFC; they plan to start farming.

TEACHING OR CRAMMING?

As far as I know, in their primary education our students were exposed to 'from the front' teaching, without much self-activity: the teacher tells a story and the children listen. Whether it originates from training or nature, I do not know, but the students have on the whole a good memory. This has its influence on the way they want to be taught. They want to get notes so that they try to master the subject matter by rote-learning. The notes are preferred in full, without tables, schedules, graphs and other schematic notation, because interpretation and reading of graphs and tables give many problems. But notes can be learned. As shown by the test results the trainees do indeed learn the notes by heart instead of trying to understand what they mean. There are exceptions of course, but most students do learn things by rote.

In my view, note learning is not very useful for future farmers. There are many protests, however, when I try to schematize the material. Graphs can only be understood by the best. This means that I can hardly use them, not even in the first phase of a lesson. To prevent students from sleeping I give them the handouts after dealing with a subject. Most students have problems filing the handouts, however, so that they can never be traced when needed, though I see some improvement in this.

So far I have had no problem choosing subjects to teach; the syllabus and my own ideas about what could be useful for future farmers give plenty of topics. The students protest, however, about the way I teach. This is mainly because of my initially basic and theoretical approach and because I integrate subjects. More than in the Netherlands, students seem to wonder, 'How can I apply this and this later?'. This causes difficulties when I start a subject with a general introduction, saving practice for a later phase. Lecturing biology, crops, horticulture, soil science and farm accounts, I have an excellent opportunity to integrate these subjects, especially using examples. This raises new objections because it appears to be confusing. Gradually, however, students seem to understand the relationship between the subjects. Integration of subject matter is essential, otherwise the different subjects will always be regarded as separate parts and consequently their practical use will be nil. Other expatriate teachers have told me that they face the same problems in secondary and professional schools.

OLD FASHIONS AND NEW METHODS

I found it difficult to teach in English, especially for the first month. Yet I refused to avoid the problem by adopting the system used by some Zambian teachers: the teacher talks for a full hour without a period of rest or interruption by the students. Students like that very much. I have not been successful in bringing an English accent into my speech. Furthermore my vocabulary is not very rich. To solve this problem I first carried a dictionary with me, but it took me too much time to look up words. Technical terms still give me problems, especially if I do not prepare well enough or when I have to change to a new subject. Some students have a good knowledge of English, however, and I have asked them to correct me if I make mistakes. In this way I try to prevent the students from copying down incorrect notes.

During practicals the students were used to working as much on their own as possible. To promote self-discipline, planning, consultation and a sense of responsibility among students, groups of five were formed with one leader to communicate between staff and the group. One group member was assigned five plots in the vegetable production unit for a week. The next week another group member was given that task on the same plots, while the whole group remained responsible, so that communication would be assured, as well as collective planning and checking. The whole idea was a flop. Nobody was willing to accept responsibility for the scheme. Every student in charge said that the other group members did not work as hard as he did, so everyone refused to work for the group and work actually came to a standstill. Besides communication within the group, planning was also poor. I can't help wonder if the Zambian has a co-operative or far more an individualistic personality. Certainly within the family structure there is a lot of co-operation, whether it is compulsory or not. There is also a sense of responsibility towards the other members of the family.

TEACHER KNOWS EVERYTHING

In secondary school, pupils have to share books, because there is not enough money to supply individual copies. In agricultural colleges like ours there is no money either, but there are no books available for our students at all. Books used in secondary schools for agricultural science can be understood by our students but these texts are too general. Then there are books that are sufficiently detailed, but they are too scientific and too difficult for our students. This forces staff members to prepare their own lectures on subjects they want to cover in lessons. That takes a lot of time, and therefore I started to write handouts on the subjects. These texts can be used more permanently.

The National Research Station, together with the Ministry of Agriculture and Water Development, has published a number of pamphlets and articles on growing crops and other subjects. This material gives a good deal of specific information. I badly needed this background information to prepare my lessons, as I was not educated in tropical agriculture. Some colleagues told me bluntly that it should not make any difference to me. According to them agriculture is agriculture, but to me there is quite a difference! If I had only been given the chance to tour the country and visit agricultural research stations and farms, then I would be able to get at least part of the knowledge and ideas I am looking for. But if one is expected to teach immediately upon arrival in a country the problem is there, especially when the teaching must be very practical. Here, a teacher is supposed to know everything. Good preparation in the country itself could help all agriculturists to make their stay more efficient.

THE TESTING DILEMMA

It is not very easy to test students' knowledge. I have tried two general testing methods, one with open questions and one with multiple choice questions. Both methods create difficulties. If only knowledge is asked for, open questions are not too bad, but if understanding is tested, results are poor. In multiple choice questions the pattern is similar, but there is an extra problem. To the students, the different solutions to the same item are too much alike, although I blame them for not reading carefully enough. However I must agree with them that the answers to my questions are much more similar than those of the multiple choice tests given by my Zambian colleagues. But I consider the answers to be so obvious that a wrong choice is pretty difficult. Many wrong choices are still made, though. The other problem the students experience in my tests is that the exercises I ask them to do in the test are apparently very different from the examples I give in my lessons. The problem dealt with is basically the same but the students only remember the example giving during my classroom-teaching.

STUDENTS' EXPECTATIONS AND REALITY

The objectives of the college and the expectations of the students do not run parallel. This is partly due to the fact that theory classes and practicals do not link up with each other or with reality. Too often training is based on unrealistic suppositions about the choices open to the new farmer. Due to a lack of finance, machinery, stock-feed, chemicals and medicines are beyond reach of the farmer-graduate. Aid given to a farmer starting up would be useful, but this is impossible because of lack of funds. Even a few bags of fertilizer and some seeds and tools could give the college-leaver some chance.

On the other hand the students expect themselves to be very skilled farmers by the time they leave the college. When I explain that the college is only giving them a start in a long process of learning this generates hilarious reactions. The certificate is regarded as proof that they know what they need to know to become successful farmers. Because of this apparent overestimation of their capacities, the settlement schemes, which are potential places for them to start farming, do not like to accept farm college graduates. These former students pretend to know everything better than the staff of the scheme, which hampers their own progress and the progress of the other farmers in the scheme as well. This conceit hinders a realistic approach towards future farming practice. At the start of the course students believe and expect to become owners of large-scale mechanized and well-staffed farms. During the course some of them begin to realize that this objective is too fantastic. As a result they get disappointed and they lose interest in the very idea of starting a farm of their own. Others go on building castles in the air. Some are more realistic, realizing the problem that capital will be. They first want to get employment for some years to save money. But saving money is a problem for many Zambians. It is difficult to do so for cultural and personal reasons, proof of which is the fact that many of them, even the well paid, are broke just before pay-day.

There is also a small group of students that want to start farming straight after they have finished the college, to expand their small holding gradually. Some of them succeed quite well. If the man wants to start in his village of origin, however, he might face some problems. He will be expected to maintain his rather extensive family, thus diminishing his chances of building up his farm. For most of the settlers this is a good reason not to go back to their homes. This raises the problem of finding a piece of land in another area and of settling down into the other society where they have no families to rely on.

THE GOLDEN MEAN

With the majority of the students, I am on the same terms I would like to be with students in the Netherlands. Some students have lost credit with me, though, because of their behaviour. They are obstinate, have a big mouth or try to get around me. With about 20 per cent of the students, mainly the ones that want to start farming after completing their study, I am on good terms. They come to visit me regularly, initially because, as they told me, they pity me because I am always alone. To them this is the same as being lonely. After some visits some of them became very demanding. They asked for drinks or they wanted to borrow money. This might be explained culturally but I have made it clear that this is not part of my culture, even though I am in Zambia. That is not understood, but it is accepted. They accept that I do not just give things, not even to people who are friendly.

I keep periodicals on agriculture at my house. These periodicals are very attractive to the students. Sometimes I give them these magazines, except the ones on farm machinery, because mechanization is beyond their reach. It only leads to day-dreams. However, I cannot make them understand what I mean. From the beginning students were not so humble with me as with my Zambian colleagues. I liked that. But gradually they have become so free that I should like them to restrict themselves a bit. Some lessons are spent on discussions about what I should and should not teach. In itself it is good that students want to express their view instead of always keeping their mouth shut, but it takes up a lot of time that could be used for other useful issues.

On training issues, I have experienced one point of disagreement with an expatriate colleague. This concerned whether or not mechanized large-scale farming should be introduced as a subject within the training programme. His opinion is that it should be introduced into the training to show our students a long-term perspective. The contrary opinion – mine – is that it should not be introduced, because the students will regard this as 'real' farming, and if this 'real' farming cannot be achieved, there will not be any farming at all! I have the same problem with Zambian colleagues. Against their better judgement they continue emphasizing 'real' farming in their lessons. Even their experiences with previous groups do not change this approach.

A last problem, which has much influence on the college as a whole, is the discord among the staff, which also affects the students and the other personnel. For years there has been a 'battle' for power that influences staffing policy, intake and assessment of students, relations between members of staff, their attitude towards students, the making of decisions and their implementation on all levels. This is the basis of the bad relationships I have with some individuals at the college. This was not a problem in the beginning because I did not understand the situation. Since then the problem has become so clear to me, however, I can clarify many previous difficulties and I really hope that it now will be easier for me to solve future problems. I am trying to find the golden mean between my own cultural and educational background and this completely new and challenging situation in Zambia.

7 BACK TO THE LAND

Ben Veldboom

CHIPEMBI FARM COLLEGE

After arriving in Zambia at Lusaka International Airport, you will find a beautiful tar road leading to the capital, twenty-five kilometres to the west. There is also a gravel road going north, with many pot-holes; it is corrugated and in the rainy season sometimes flooded. A jolting fifty-two kilometre ride over a bumpy road will bring you to Chipembi Farm College, a peaceful place in a farming area far away from the city.

Early this century, Methodist missionaries in the district noticed the great need for agricultural training. The Chipembi Mission Farm was then founded, to demonstrate better farming methods to churchmen and villagers. This became Chipembi Farm College in 1964, when it was opened as a private institution under the United Church of Zambia. Students were recruited from all over the country. The Zambian Government expected Chipembi Farm College to play a very important part of the country's agrarian revolution by training young Zambians as farmers. Therefore the college was awarded a considerable annual grant. Since its start over 500 students have passed through the college. The majority have returned to the land.

Yearly, over 1000 young people apply for this course, of which only thirty-five can be accepted. The entrance requirements are: age between twenty-two and thirty-five years, minimum education of seven classes of primary schools, and maximum education of Form three of secondary school. The duration of the course is two years. Each class has about thirty students.

The weekly programme for students is:
– *Fifteen hours theory in the classroom.* The subjects studied are crop husbandry, horticulture, animal husbandry, farm machinery, farm accounts and management.
– *Fifteen hours practical work and practical training.* To support itself the college has several production units for crops, horticulture, beef-cattle and poultry. During the practicals, students do the work. In this way they are trained in the production units, and the workshop section as well.
– *Fifteen hours gardening.* Every student has a garden of about 500 square metres, where he grows vegetables under instruction. Seeds, fertilizers and chemicals are bought from the college and the vegetables are sold in Lusaka. Some

students make more than K 400[1] profit per year from their plots. This money can be used as an initial downpayment on their future farms.

I started working at the college as an instructor, but later I took on some administrative duties as well. The total number of instructors and administrative staff is 10, and there are 15 general workers in the sections. In the past there were sometimes more than five expatriate staff, but nowadays this college is more Zambianized. After my departure, in June 1981, there were only two expatriate instructors left. They are sponsored by the Organization of Netherlands Volunteers. There is sufficient qualified Zambian staff for these posts, but the college cannot afford to pay all their salaries. The annual grant has decreased while all costs have gone up excessively. This is mostly due to the difficult economic situation in Zambia. The country's economy mainly depends on the copper industry, which has slumped because of low market prices. To reduce dependance on food imports and improve the balance of payments the government is trying to stimulate food production by all means. One of their incentives is to train young people as farmers at institutions such as Chipembi Farm College. People are encouraged to go back to the land and to produce more food for the nation.

WORKING IN AN OTHER COUNTRY IS LIVING WITH ITS PEOPLE

Standing for the first time in front of a class of thirty students, I felt it was impossible to learn everyone's name. Not only did all the faces look the same to me, but all the names also seemed to be similar, and they were difficult to pronounce. Besides that, it was a problem to distinguish the christian names and surnames. When working with people it is important to know them and to know how to pronounce their names. I, too, appreciate that people I meet everyday know how to address me. Students in Zambia are usually older than those I used to teach in Holland. Some of them may even be older than their instructors. In the beginning, it is not easy to estimate their age, but it is important to know how old your students are, since older students should always be approached with more respect.

The expatriate's relationship with his counterpart will partly depend on the experience of the counterpart as compared with that of the expatriate. My counterpart accepted my guidance easily, not only because I had been posted above him, but also because he expected that I had more knowledge than he, so he could learn something from me. Besides, there is always respect for someone coming from Western countries, which is undoubtedly inherited from colonial days. An African is in general very polite, he will never disappoint you. When you ask him to show you the way, he will always direct you somewhere, even when he is not sure about it himself. The same applies to the students and the counterpart: they will give you the answer that they think you expect from

1 US $1.00 = 0.79 kwacha; 1 kwacha = 100 ngwee.

them. It is difficult to discover what they really think. If they have a complaint or when they disagree with you, they will not come straight out with it; you will hear about it from others sometime later.

My counterpart had been at the college already for about one year when I arrived, and he was more experienced than me in some subjects, e.g. in growing tropical crops. He had worked with my predecessor, who was more experienced than me. Therefore the counterpart had great expectations from me also, which I could not always live up to.

I want to say a few words about personnel matters. When participating in the management of the college I realized that it was hard for me to deal with personnel matters. Rules for recruitment, salary level, leave, etc. are quite vague. It was difficult to find out which criteria are used in cases of dismissal. Warnings only have value when they are in writing. It is also important to know that it is very usual to order someone to do a job that is not within his field. In my opinion it is better not to become involved in personnel matters.

In the past many experts from different countries have come to work at the college. After a few years, they leave again. For the Zambian instructors it must be difficult to work with such a variety of people, all of whom bring with them their different views. When submitting new ideas, it is often hard to convince colleagues of your views. One reason is that they have already seen various ideas fail soon after they were put into effect. It is better first to settle at the project and discover how the present system works. Only then will it be possible to discuss changes with your counterpart and other colleagues. It is important to remember that they have to continue working with the system after you have left.

Coming into a new area, it is always advisable to make contact with the local authorities. For the college, this is the Board of Governors; in the village, the village-headman or chief; and in a district, the police officers and also party officials. Sometimes they need your help; sometimes you need their help. During a time of political friction I was suspected of espionage, but after I consulted some of the local authorities it was found that it was all based on mis-understandings. Not only in such an awkward situation, but also in others, it is good to have known them before. When visiting a village, you should always first go to greet the village headman; he will show you his village, his people and many other interesting things.

GIVE ME TWO NGWEE

Children usually speak only the local language, but when they see a *musungu* (European) they can muster a little English: 'Give me two ngwee'. The child expects that all white people are rich. This symbolizes the difference between rich and poor, which is here much bigger than in Western countries. For example, in the college there are low class, paid employees and middle class, paid employees: the salary of the middle class group is ten times higher than that of the low class. I have the same housing facilities and salary as my colleagues. The only difference is that they have more commitments, such as taking care of parents and other relatives. While I regard my house as being big enough for me, they prove that it is possible to live with fifteen people in a similar house. I am able to use a car; they are not. Such status also means that I am not supposed to charge passengers when giving them a lift to town.

'Excuse me sir, I have a very big problem'. This always is the introduction for a request for financial help. It may vary from a small amount to buy some bread to a large amount as a grant for planting a hectacre of maize. You are asked for help because they know you have got more than they have. The explanation that their own salary is not sufficient mostly appears to be true. And then it is difficult to refuse, unless the amount is too high or when there is no security for repayment.

There seems to be a permanent shortage of commodities like sugar, salt and soap, but often they are still available in the homes of expatriates. When these items are in the shops, the expatriate has the transport and the cash to buy up a good stock. Granting requests for these items, however, usually results in more and more requests, without solving the real problem.

SORRY SIR, TRY NEXT WEEK

Not only people have financial problems, organizations can be broke too. Every training institution needs money, and so does the farm college. The annual grant we received from the government was just sufficient to pay all the staff salaries. This meant that the money for education material, spares and maintenance had to come from other sources. In my introductory words I touched on the difficult economic situation in Zambia. There is no sign that the annual grant will be increased soon, but all costs go up at least once a year. Besides, taking receipt of the money is often a complicated procedure. You have to contact various offices, only to hear finally 'Sorry sir, try next week'. Sometimes this procedure has to be repeated several times. And then, when you have money and you try to buy books, spares or other things, you will often hear 'Try next week'. In some cases an expatriate will be more successful in buying these items. It may also be easier to get money and materials from overseas. But I have doubts about whether I should use my position in such a way.

We received money from several sponsoring organizations overseas for a number of sub-projects. It should not be too difficult to control the spending of the money. But what do you do when this money arrives, while at the same moment there is not a single *ngwee* for recurrent expenditure at the college? Usually the money will be used 'temporarily' for recurrent purposes, with the intention of transferring this sum to the sub-project later, when there is more cash available. Of course this is not always possible and therefore it is difficult to check whether all money has reached its intended destination. There is plenty of money in Western countries available to sponsor projects in developing countries. The problem is, however, where to spend it and how to spend it.

Sponsoring organizations are also creating various opportunities for scholarships in Western countries. Where this is within the scope of agriculture, I should like to make one more comment. All circumstances in Africa, such as climate, infra-structure and market, are totally different from the European situation. Besides that, the participant will be confronted with modern equipment that he will not be able to use in his own country. When he tries to do so, he will realize that it is not available. If it is available, it will often be too expensive. I received several requests from my students to organize such a scholarship for them, but I find it rather difficult to decide whether to go on organizing courses or to advise a scholarship, either in the student's own country or in other tropical countries.

ONE ZAMBIA, ONE NATION

In Zambia there are seven different languages and even more tribes. Yet there is one political party, the United National Independence Party. The national slogan is: One Zambia! One Nation! Politics has little influence on the daily management of the college, although on official occasions it may happen that everyone needs a day off to participate. Also, the college tractors and the lorry may be used for transport and other preparations. In such cases mileage cannot be claimed. The first time I saw this happening, I raised some questions. It was explained to me that this was one of the usual services to the nation; in fact, the college has always been supported by national grants. The political ideal 'back to the land' is of course in complete agreement with the college's aim of training young people to be farmers.

SOME CULTURAL ASPECTS

Before entering a new and unknown community it is important to learn something about its culture, but it will only be possible to understand some of its aspects after living there for a longer period.

In Zambia the official language is English, but there are several main local languages that are still very important. Upon arriving in the country I realized that my English was still poor. Moreover, I had a Dutch accent, my pronunciation being quite different to that heard in Zambia.

It was interesting to realize that the letter r does not exist in some local languages (nor do q, v, x and z). Instead of r, the l is used, and as a result in Zambian English r and l are always mixed up. This sometimes results in some funny words. Invited for a meal, I was told that we would be eating *lice*. Another time when I asked a student where he kept his certificates, he answered: 'Well sir, I *fired* them all'! And each year when the rainy season starts, the air is full of *frying-ants*, which will be tastily prepared in the *flying-pan*.

The people are more consequent in their use of English than we are. When a student is asked, 'Have you done your homework?', he may answer 'No sir'. If asked again, 'You have not done it?', he will say, 'Yes sir!' This means, 'Yes sir, I have *not* done it!'. It is advisable to avoid a question beginning with 'Haven't you'.

Christianity is spread all over the country, but the influence of old, local religions is still quite important. When something inexplicable or unusual happens, it must be because of spirits. One may not be able to perform his duties because of spirits and witchcraft. This may even result in resignations of students or staff. It is difficult to do anything because Europeans are said to be immune to such powers. The situation does not apply to them.

Eating customs are also interesting to learn about. A guest should never refuse an invitation to eat with his host; it would be an insult. Usually the men and guests will eat first and later on the women and children. The staple food in Zambia is *nshima*, a stiff maize-meal porridge. The main protein source is groundnuts, and, if available, chicken or dried fish. Various agronomists have tried to introduce crops such as soya beans, which could serve as an additional protein supply, but here a problem arises. Soya beans are also used as feed for cattle and pigs. And one should not recommend that animal fodder be used for human consumption. Conversely maize should not be recommended for feeding animals, because maize is a staple food for humans.

Also, it is important never to violate a person's sense of justice. When it is necessary to punish someone, be sure which words are acceptable and which words should never be used. It is also a great mistake to punish someone or to point out his mistakes in the presence of others. To do so in front of the offender's subordinates is even worse.

The influence of our own culture on the local community culture is not easy to estimate, but it is certainly great. Everything we bring with us, such as a radio, cassette recorder, camera, watch and clothes, are articles in great demand but short supply. The result is prices are very high. Soon after I arrived at the college, I received 'reservations' for my boots and jeans (which were worn out when my contract was over). Probably these problems are more serious in Zambia than elsewhere, mainly because many articles have to be imported, which involves high transport costs and import duties. However, all these goods have been in the country for years and they are displayed in the shops. Therefore in my opinion there is no reason for a development worker to try to live here as a very poor man. It would be hypocritical, since everyone knows that when the expatriate returns to his country he will again enjoy 'wealth' and 'luxury' just as he did before.

TRAINING SCHOOL-LEAVERS TO BE FARMERS

'Training school-leavers to be farmers' is the shortest description of the aim of Chipembi Farm College. It is a very valuable and useful aim, but at the same time a difficult and complicated one, with many different aspects to it.

School-leavers, as already mentioned, may have completed Grade Seven of primary school, while others have completed Form Three, a difference of three years of secondary-school education. In addition, the level of teaching in schools in the bush cannot be compared with that of schools in the city. Schools in the bush often have problems getting staff, as well as teaching materials. As a result there is an enormous hetrogeneity among the students at the college, which is quite a problem since all students follow the same syllabus. There are about thirty students in each course year; by Zambian standards this is a small class. Therefore there is no convincing reason to split up the class into two or more different levels. Besides, students will not accept being placed in the lower group. To solve the problem of the groups being too heterogeneous, I was intending to make some special material for more advanced students. Also, when teaching certain subjects I have tried to split the class, giving tasks to smaller groups of students. This requires good preparation by the teacher, because the students are not used to it.

There is not much known about the syllabi of the various schools the students have previously attended. Anyway, some students are even thirty-five years (and over) old. They finished primary school about twenty years ago. Obviously the syllabi were different then. This lack of knowledge about the educational background of each student is another problem to be met in teaching. Suggestions were made to concentrate on either Grade Seven or Form Three leavers. This idea was rejected because both groups are more or less drop-outs. It is very difficult for them to find other venues for further education except at this college.

The educational needs of the students (prospective farmers) are not very clear. One will start growing crops, while another will concentrate on livestock. Students expect to become commercial farmers but their circumstances vary widely: some commercial farms are ten hectares while others are more than a hundred hectares. It would be useful to look at the employment histories of the 500 students who have passed through this college in the last seventeen years. Unfortunately there is no clear record. Some have become prosperous commercial farmers, while others have gone back to their jobs as *mishanga boys* (cigarette-sellers at the market) or taxi drivers. It is believed, however, that the majority returned to the land. Some are big commercial farmers, others have small-scale farms in a farmers settlement scheme or work on a co-operative farm. Quite a number have found employment as farm managers, section managers or general labourers on farms. Again, it is not easy to distill from all these types of farm work the educational needs of the majority.

Apparently there had never been a complete, written syllabus or curriculum at this college. I was given the task of writing a new syllabus and curriculum. In my opinion it is very important to have a syllabus and curriculum, otherwise nobody knows where to start and where to end. The main and most important problem is to find out which subjects should be in the syllabus. Another important element is that theory and practical instruction should link up. This means that when doing the seasonal practical work, the relevant theory should also be covered. As I have already mentioned, apart from receiving practical instruction students work in the college production unit. In return they are given a monthly living allowance.

The college does not have many textbooks for its students. It is difficult to find books that match the level of the course and its specific character. And if they are available, they are often too expensive. Usually lectures are written by the teacher and duplicated for students.

We had an overhead projector, which can be very useful because the quality of blackboards and chalk is poor. Besides, with an overhead projector it is easy to run over previous lessons, which I find very important here. It is a pity, however, that until now the overhead projector has only been used by expatriate staff. Another disadvantage is that all ancilliary equipment, such as transparant sheets, markers and spare bulbs, still has to come from Europe.

There are not many models or other teaching aids available, but it is always possible to give a demonstration during practical lessons. I found the practical instruction to be very useful, because it is done in small groups. Most lecturers are not used to teaching practicals, however.

In the beginning I found it hard to get used to the particular technical terminology in English. For instance, I did not have much knowledge about tropical crops, so tuition on these crops was done by other lecturers more experienced in these subjects. I taught the more general subjects, such as botany, soils and fertilizers.

When interviewing applicants for the course it is remarkable how high their expectations are. Some of them expect to have a farm of hundreds of hectares of land with many cattle and pigs or poultry. When asked where they will get the money from to do so, the answer usually is: 'a loan from the bank or the government', or 'the college will help me'. During most of the lectures on farm management I have to spend time explaining that the college cannot help them so much and that neither the bank nor the government will give them such a loan unless they have security. These false expectations probably arise from the college advertisement, which says: 'Training young people to be commercial farmers'. 'Commercial' may also apply to a small farm, however, but the fallacy arises when they think of the large scale mechanized farms, which are often run by Europeans. Obviously, someone who is inexperienced will not be able to run such a farm after only two years of training. It is hard to explain to students that this is a delusion and that they first have to start working by hand or use oxen. Fortunately, by the time they graduate they have all learned to lower their expectations. Nevertheless it would be better not to use the word 'commercial' in the college advertisements.

The motivation of students is good, as can be seen from the high number of applicants for this course, so you would expect that discipline should not be a problem. Yet rules for students are in my opinion quite authoritarian, which the local teachers believe to be necessary, even though most of the students are adults; some are even older than their instructors. The end result is sometimes friction, particularly when it comes to the compulsory practical duties in the college production units. It is good to take account of differences in age. As I have already mentioned, an adult should be approached with more respect. The community has quite a clear view about whether one is a grown-up or still a 'young chap'. For me it was always a problem to estimate peoples ages.

Tests and exams are mainly on theory. Due to the heterogeneity of ability within the groups, the results vary enormously. This makes it difficult to find an objective standard. I suggested more testing of practical work, which would give those with less education a better chance.

Students attach much value to the college certificate. Usually, all students receive a certificate if they behave well and work well during the practicals. They attach even more value to certificates from foreign countries. Students have the possibility of sitting for exams from a training institution in the U.K. I have some objections to this form of education, because it is not based on the practical situation of the students. They just study to pass their exam, even when they have to learn about camels and donkeys, which they have never seen and will never work with.

For teaching staff, courses in didactics should be organized, because most instructors have no didactic or pedagogical training. For this reason most of them have no variety of teaching methods to use during their lectures.

I noticed a difference in motivation between expatriate staff and Zambian staff. Expatriate staff often teach with a lot of energy and enthusiasm, probably because they come with a certain aim in mind. This attitude is not usually found amongst Zambian colleagues. For them, teaching is mainly a way of earning a living. It would be an advantage, however, if this attitude could be more often combined with an energetic and enthusiastic approach.

PROBLEMS AND REWARDS

So far I have written about the main problems that I met in the three years I spent at Chipembi Farm College. Of course, there were also many rewards and good experiences. Describing these could also easily fill ten pages or more, but this was not what was asked of me. However, I suspect that some references to my good experiences can be found in my account. Certainly the most stimulating aspect of my stay in Zambia was my being able to contribute towards the colleges aim: training people to farm the land. If Chipembi Farm College continues to be properly managed and run with zeal, it will be able to go on training many people who will go back to the land to produce more food for their country.

8   THIS IS MY HAND AND THIS IS MY HEAD

Willem Zijp

THE JOB

The multi-donor Basic Agricultural Services Programme was started in Lesotho in 1978. Its general aims are to strengthen the Ministry of Agriculture there and to bring about an increase in the production of the main food crops. An important component of the programme is training, which is funded by the World Bank. In particular, the programme aims to increase the output of general purpose extension workers by thirty persons each year for the duration of the programme (five years). To provide the training a branch of the Lesotho Agricultural College was established at Leribe.

The objective of the training is to produce young men and women who will go out into the field as General Purpose Extension Assistants. Thus, extension is a vitally important part of the course. However when I arrived in Lesotho I discovered that very little extension was being taught (thirty-eight periods in the two-year course) at the main branch of the college, in the capital, Maseru. I was asked to write an extension syllabus for about 350 periods. Although I found this a great challenge, I regretted not having a counterpart extension lecturer. This gave me much freedom, though, and I was able to write a programme that I considered most suited to the training needs of the students.

It was evident from the start that the training provided in Maseru is not very practical and it is doubtful if the training suits the job of an extension assistant. The extension course at Leribe has three distinct components:
– theory, including some lectures about communication, learning, change, adoption of new ideas, some role plays, etc.,
– practicals, during which the students visit a neighbouring village one day per week to do some extension work,
– vacation work, during which the students spend three of their vacation periods in extension training. The students are required to:
· make a survey of their own,
· spend five weeks in the field with an experienced, reliable extension assistant,
· give a number of demonstrations.
The practicals and vacations, in particular, are very popular with students, and so far the Leribe graduates have done very well in this way.

What follows is a description of the problems I have as a teacher, but I would like to stress that teaching is not entirely problematic, it is also a source of

satisfaction. Development and execution of the extension syllabus gives me great pleasure, as does co-operation with my counterpart extension lecturer, who has now joined the staff.

THE SOCIAL CONTEXT

A rather unique feature of Lesotho is its location within the Republic of South Africa. Leribe is only a small village. There are no sports facilities except for a muddy tennis court, and shopping is extremely limited. So we do our shopping in South Africa, about twenty kilometres away. I also play squash there. It is only a small consolation to know that whatever we buy in Lesotho is imported by Indian traders from South Africa anyway, so buying across the border only reduces the middle man's profit. Still it is an ambivalent feeling to go to the 'Land of Apartheid' to do your shopping.

I am very fortunate that in the three years of my stay in Lesotho I have never encountered real social problems. My relations with colleagues and neighbours, expatriates and locals, have always been subtle and easy-going, though rather superficial. Outside work I find it difficult to have a profound relationship with any of the local colleagues. After many attempts, I have found that a meaningful talk is a rare phenomenon anyway and that social evenings, like cocktail parties, do not really help one to develop deeper relations with others. This means that in a relatively remote place as Leribe, where I live with my wife and our child, you have to take a lot of initiatives yourself. There are virtually no outside stimuli and this can put a strain on people. In the beginning this situation did not bother us but it became increasingly difficult the longer we stayed. The lack of interesting things outside our own small family clearly put our relationship under stress. Fortunately this has resulted in an even stronger bond between us, but there were times that the very continuation of our relationship was at stake.

We particularly missed advice from friends, and even more so from two grandmothers – strange at it may sound – on how to cope with our new-born baby. How do you distinguish crying because of hunger from crying because of a dirty nappy or boredom? Learning how to fold a nappy from a diagram in a book is certainly possible, but I am sure that grandmothers know little practical tricks to make life a lot easier. However interesting we found the way the Basotho guide and coach their children, we still felt the urge to talk with someone from a more comparable background.

The different behaviour of the various groups of colleagues has also created some inconvenience. I find it essential to try and find out exactly what people expect of you when they invite you out. It is also very important to know what to do if you invite other people.

My wife and I were once invited as the only non-Britishers to an all-English Christmas dinner. We were very pleased with the invitation and had planned to dress up for the occasion. At half past two in the afternoon our host came by when we were working in our new garden to ask what kept us so long. Little did we know that the English eat Christmas dinner at lunch-time!

If you invite Basotho to a party, some of them tend to drink a fair bit more than is good for them. On a number of occasions we have had to carry some of the guests home. Sometimes they even slept in the garden and left the next morning. If this was the only problem it wouldn't be so bad but unfortunately some people when drunk become rather obnoxious and harass the women.

Some people I know, expatriate and local, only display a small quantity of drinks and wait to serve any further rounds of alcohol or food until after the worst boozers have left. Clearly there is a risk that the people who come to enjoy the party will leave as well. I am afraid I still have not found a satisfactory equilibrium between the expectations of hospitality of the guests, on the one side, and their excessive use of alcohol, on the other.

MATERIAL PROBLEMS

Lesotho is a mountainous kingdom, slightly smaller than the Netherlands, and completely landlocked by the Republic of South Africa. It is therefore natural that apartheid and its inequalities are constantly on people's minds. I was therefore amazed and embarrassed to find that the houses of expatriate staff and local staff are not only different in size of garden and number of rooms. The houses of expatriates are whitewashed, while the local staff quarters are built in a dark-brownish brick. My local colleagues made no secret of their dislike of this situation and all staff members asked the responsible person in the central government if at least their walls could be painted white and trees planted. In no uncertain terms we were told that, with the future in mind, the government had decided to build the houses exactly as they were. These houses were to be let to local government personnel after the termination of the project and we should understand that among them there are people of many different ranks and they would require different types of housing. Not a very good start for me, but at least I was able to show my good-will by starting the ball rolling. It struck me at the time, however, that although local staff members felt rather strongly about the matter, they did not take any action. I have experienced this on many occasions.

Another material problem I encountered in the beginning and continue to encounter is transport, or rather the lack of it. At first I would go to the transport officer and ask, for instance, 'Can I have a car next Thursday at 9 a.m.?' Invariably the answer would be 'yes'. Just as invariably, the car would not be there. It took me some time to find out that the man did not dare to say 'sorry, all cars are booked for Thursday but it will be all right on Wednesday or Friday' because he did not want to offend me by giving me what he considered to be a rude answer. Consequently he would always answer in the affirmative. It would have been better to ask 'are any cars available next Thursday at 9 a.m.?'. This question is not so personal, but still the person answering would prefer to give an affirmation. I find that I can never find the right question for all situations. To make sure my name was on the transport list, I took some extra time to formulate my request more carefully. An opening question could be, for instance, 'Next week I would like to go to X, what would be the best day, do you think' and go from there.

Talking about time, I always take into consideration that it takes at least a few hours to get started on any job. When I want to show a film you can bet that the lamp is broken and that I will have to replace it. When I was typing this very story I had to repair the typewriter before I could start. Last week I wanted to cut some grass with the tractor and mower. I had to fix both before I could start. A complete list of this kind of occurrence would be endless.

The people actually operating the machinery are not always to blame, either. I have found that operators, drivers and labourers are extremely willing and eager to learn. Teaching them is not wasted time. I have found on many occasions that drivers do not have the slightest idea about the engine under the bonnet of the car they have been driving for years. They are supposed to maintain their vehicles but during a training session it became clear that the drivers did not know what the radiator was for, nor did they know why they had to pour water rather than oil or petrol in it. One should not be surprised when people put diesel fuel in a petrol-engined car, as has indeed happened a number of times.

ME AND THE PROJECT

When I started as a teacher in Leribe in December 1978 I had spent a year in the country on another project and I had already discovered that careful planning and organization were not the strongest points of my local colleagues. (Yet the avoidable mistakes made in the initial stages of the project were made by the expatriate donors.) This project has five vehicles, none of which is suited to my needs, to carry about twenty students twice a week via very bad roads to some nearby villages. None of the vehicles can carry more than a ton, which is very awkward for the livestock people, who have to transport large quantities of feed over considerable distances, let alone animals.

The audio-visual aids, which were ordered before the arrival of any of the trainers, are completely unsuited for the job. As repairs are difficult to organize and some of the spare parts are virtually unobtainable, many of these sophisticated aids are standing idle. I can see a reason for the bad purchasing policies, though. The selection and allocation of expatriate staff is extremely time-consuming. If a project was to wait until all members of staff arrive, much valuable time would be lost because the ordering of the necessary equipment will also take disproportionally much time in relation to the total duration of the project. Nevertheless you can't help asking yourself if it wouldn't be better to organize the selection and allocation of expatriate staff more smoothly in the first place and to accept as a fact that development co-operation is a long-term affair and that things take time.

Another very important aspect of project policy I still have problems with is the counterpart system as it is executed here. Upon arrival at the college I met my counterpart extension lecturer. We worked well together for about a month, but then he left for Canada for further training. I worked on my own for about a year and although that arrangement is relatively free and easy, I do not consider it ideal at all. After a year a local extension trainer joined the staff and I am very glad to say we get on well together. However the person who is now in Canada will return to his job in this project. By that time not only will I leave but, as the policy now stands, also my current counterpart. So the training of counterpart staff on the spot will not benefit the project. My counterpart and I have organized many things, while the man in Canada does not know anything of the first attempts at teaching extension at Leribe. We try to keep as many records as possible of our experiences, achievements and failures but I am afraid that we are the only ones who do so. Even obvious records like crop yields, planting dates and fertilizer rates are not or only erratically kept. Somehow nobody seems capable of writing down exactly what happened and nobody is really interested in doing so either. This manifests itself clearly in most of our meetings, when the college chairman consistently asks, 'What do you intend to do next month?'. But I have never heard him say, 'What did you do last month?'.

Evaluation of personal achievement is looked at askance. A test is not meant to assess both teacher's and student's progress; in the opinion of both local staff and students it is only a punishment. In the same vein, the Lesotho Agricultural College has no knowledge about the whereabouts of her graduates whatsoever. I am pleased that lately there seems to be a change in this attitude: more records are now being kept. Probably this is due to some of the donor countries requiring reliable data on which to base their aid programmes.

When I arrived at the Leribe Training Centre, in December 1978, the place was still called the Farmers Training Centre. The centre was selected to accommodate the northern branch of the Lesotho Agricultural College. The power struggle between the resident officer of the Farmers Training Centre and the director of the college that followed caused an enormous waste of time, effort, money and good-will. I scrupulously tried to steer clear of their continuing quarrels but every now and then I found myself mixed up in one of their disputes.

> I remember being asked to leave a hall, where I was showing a film to students for their entertainment, because I had not asked the resident officer permission to use the hall. The fact that I had invited him to attend that afternoon did not mean a thing, the students and I had to leave. Even now, almost a year later, they struggle on. Clearly, nobody seems able to take a decision as to who is now in charge of the place.

This is only one example of the inability to make decisions when it concerns people of similar rank. This is in sharp contrast with the situation when people of different ranks are concerned, for example, teachers are right and students

90

are wrong. Students are sometimes even referred to as 'children', even though their ages vary from 18 to 26. Some of the staff deny them the most elementary rights and take far-reaching decisions without careful consideration. Again, it is significant that in the original plan of the college premises no facilities were provided for the recreation of students. As it was, the only thing the students could do was watch the traffic go by, and there is not even much of that. It has taken me almost one-and-a-half years to get only the meagrest of facilities organized, but then most local staff members consider money spent on recreation for the students as a waste.

POLITICS AND PATRONAGE

When I joined FAO I had to promise that I would abstain from politics in the country I was going to work in. I do exactly that and I have no real problems as such. The difficulty is that on many occasions people try to force you to take sides. As in many other countries, in Lesotho there is a tendency to appoint certain people to positions of authority, but not because of their capabilities. Their political background is taken into disproportionate consideration. In contrast, very able people in some cases are promoted rather slowly. It is more difficult to work with people who have been promoted very quickly, especially when this promotion is not because of their performance.

> I was once reprimanded by a superior officer whose main contribution to agriculture was his relationship to a high government official. I received this rebuke for bringing back a Landrover dirty after a days driving along bad, muddy tracks. He told me I was wasting money because somebody had to be paid to clean the vehicle.

> Then there is an incident that happened during a big hay-baling campaign. Everything and everybody was ready – no mean feat in itself. Rain was threatening to fall and spoil the hay. Unfortunately the string used in the balers was locked away in the cupboard of the campaign leader. The whole campaign was postponed and the hay was spoiled just because the leader of the campaign did not show up for work for a couple of days. No reason for his absence was given.

I commented upon the man's behaviour in rather strong terms. A local friend of mine came to our house later to talk to me. While he completely agreed with me about this person he strongly advised me to keep quiet as he also had done. A very close relative of the man in question was a 'big shot' in the government. Needless to say it was this relative that got him the job in the first place. However difficult it was for me to accept, I took my friend's advice. At the same time I realized that I had witnessed an unexpected problem: a huge communication gap between local officers. I have encountered difficulties many times because of this lack of communication between people of different political backgrounds. Some colleagues have even told me, 'We don't like the government, so why should we do our best in our work?'. When I asked them why they worked for the government in the first place, they answered that they needed a job and there are not many alternatives. I am glad to report that in the recent decentralization in Lesotho very competent people have been put in charge of the districts. They know the problems and they are honest about them, which makes life a lot easier.

EGGS AND APPLES: CULTURAL ISSUES

Language, apart from being an extremely fascinating object of study, can be a source of misunderstandings.

How does the following question and answer strike you? Typically I could ask, 'Didn't you spread any fertilizer on this piece of land?'. The student may answer 'yes', which means that he didn't. Logically speaking the student is right, but I would be at a complete loss. What did he mean? Did he or did he not spread fertilizer? To avoid this I have learned to always ask my questions in the affirmative form: 'Did you spread fertilizer on this field?'. The student can then answer yes or no and I will understand that straightforward answer. The fact that the answer will probably be, 'Maybe . . . I don't know exactly, sir' is not really a language problem.

Some of the students' English is rather poor, especially when they arrive at the college. This combined with their initial shyness, their acute realization of cultural differences with fellow students, local teachers and expatriates does not help to generate an easy-going learning situation. The authoritative way Basotho are taught at most mission schools does not create an atmosphere in which students get the best chance to improve their English either. Nevertheless they seem to pick up enough English to understand the lectures and demonstrations sufficiently. Moreover I must admit that their English is a lot better than my Sesotho.

When I arrived in Lesotho I was made to understand that my contract would not be for more than one year. I did not feel one year was worth the trouble of learning a relatively minor language. Moreover it was a language that I never expected to have to use again. Swahili or Hausa are languages spoken by much larger groups of people and are probably worth learning even if one plans to stay only one year. I have been here now four years and they have asked me to stay another year after completion of my present contract. I have learned to greet people in Sesotho and to ask the way, but I have never really sat down to learn Sesotho seriously. However I can say in fluent Sesotho that I don't understand Sesotho. Uttering this learnt-by-heart phrase always causes a lot of misunderstanding, because if you don't speak Sesotho, how can you say that so proficiently in Sesotho? It does help to break the ice though.

Part of my lectures are about culture. It always strikes me that the few students who have heard about history are quick with their verdicts when asked about the original population of Lesotho, the San (Bushmen): 'They don't have any culture, sir.' I then make an effort to demonstrate to them that not only do

92

the San have an extremely complex and sophisticated culture, but also that culture is not only the 'classic stuff' like paintings, music, literature, but their whole way of life: what you eat, how you eat and when you eat is as much a part of your culture as your music.

Students were always utterly amazed when I told them that in the Netherlands people hang a snake-like fish (eel) in the smoke of a fire and that they actually eat the animal. Elsewhere in Africa I almost caused some people to retch when I used my handkerchief. They found it already rather strange that I used a piece of material to blow my nose, but they turned away in disgust when they saw me put the dirty wad into my pocket. They of course blow their noses by blocking one nostril and blowing hard through the other.

There are so many examples. Imagine what they think of people whose hands are so mucky that they need metal tools to eat with, rather than carefully washing their hands before dinner and using them. The extra dimension of eating with one's fingers that is added to a good meal with friends has to be forfeited by people insisting on eating with knives and forks.

Eggs are a rather special case. I believe in many African countries people attribute all sorts of power to eggs. In many cases these powers have something to do with fertility. In Lesotho girls are, traditionally, not allowed to eat eggs, as this might make them infertile.

Not knowing this, I once encouraged a group of students to start a young farmers' club in a nearby village. The main activity of that club was to have been the keeping of chickens and the sale of eggs. The whole establishment of the club went very awkwardly compared to getting similar clubs off the ground. Only after careful probing with the help of my counterpart did I find out that the parents did not want to pay the membership fee if girls were allowed to eat eggs.

I suggested to the students that they abandon the idea and start another club, which they did, but I am still not sure if that was the right advice. I did not want to aggrieve the parents, but in my opinion culture is not static, it continually changes. Was not it better to try and change part of the culture then and there, through my students? This is a very difficult question. There is an extremely delicate equilibrium between leaving people in their traditional state and helping them to change, to build for a more progressive future with sufficient food of good quality for everybody. I am sure one should not push too hard, that would only be counter-productive. But the process of development must begin somewhere otherwise the gap between rich and poor will widen.

In this respect, I believe that I may claim the right to help create changes in the first place. For I am in Lesotho upon invitation of the government to train (= change) students in extension (= change). Some of the farmers I work with, however, do not care a fig about the government and they take me at face value. If they like my ideas they will try them, if not they won't. And that is that.

I shall give another example to demonstrate my view.

Traditionally in Lesotho one does not talk about sexuality. My vacation programme was seriously hampered by the fact that three single female students got pregnant. I talked with all three and neither of them wanted the child. Abortion is out of the question in Lesotho, although some girls get such a severe beating at home as a punishment that they sometimes abort spontaneously. When the local matron and I suggested to the director that we should invite the existing family-planning unit to give a talk to our students he initially refused. He was afraid of the parents' anger. The matron and I persevered, arguing that there was no need to tell the parents about our plans, and that the students learn so many revolutionary things at the college that their parents would disagree with. We reached the compromise that the unit would come, give a talk, but would not mention contraceptives. In my opinion this was a very unsatisfactory solution, so I saw the matron and the district nurse privately. It was agreed that students could get contraceptives without anybody knowing.

It was not so much that tradition and modern times are very different that irritated me, but that most of the local teachers (all male) denied there was a problem in the first place. For them, if the students are ordered not to mix, its unthinkable that they will. That's that. I also get easily irritated by flagrant examples of discrimination, and the male Basotho often make me angry by the way they treat their wives.

Cultural obstacles can affect farming, too.
In 1960 an average yield of 5.6 bags of maize per acre was realized. Now it has decreased to about 2.6. Something needs to be done fast. However about 45% of the male working population works in South Africa. If I give some advice to their wives, who have to work the fields, they have to send letters to their husbands asking consent for even the simplest decision. Many times the absentee farmer writes his wife not to undertake anything until he comes back on leave, in six months time.

Farming often demands quick action and that part of the culture will have to change in this respect. It is even more of a pity when one realizes that these women are in many cases good, progressive farmers. I find it a real pleasure to work with widows: they have the status of a married woman, they sometimes even get a small pension, but they are not hamstrung by an absentee husband.

During occasional evaluation meetings the students and I discuss this. We also discuss the fact that on the whole our female students are doing better than the males. The men have rather chauvinistic ideas: the situation in Lesotho is as bad as it is because Eve ate the apple. I have heard a man say in earnest that 'woman is the root of all evil'. I find it a problem to remain calm and respectful on this point. I also find it a problem that my local colleagues do not really agree with me. They might say during discussions that emancipation is booming in Africa, but in their homes things remain as they were. But then again, how many so-called emancipated men in the West change their baby's nappies or clean the toilet?

Thank goodness for human contact that bridges the race gap.
One day we discovered that many students and staff were eating fruit from the orchard. I was told by the offenders that they were not stealing

because 'they were picking the fruit in broad daylight, so that everybody could see them'. The local farm manager and I decided to spray the whole orchard with clean water, while covering ourselves in heavy protective clothing, masks, gloves, etc. Afterwards we let it be known that the trees had been sprayed with an unusually high dose of metasystox, an extremely dangerous poison. Everybody was warned not to eat any of the lethal fruits. In fact, nobody did for quite some time. The manager and I had a lot of fun and this helped bridge the many cultural differences between us.

TEACHING, TESTING AND OTHER TRAGEDIES

What do you do when the students express their preference for you as entertainment co-ordinator and during the first election for prefect, librarian, football coach, etc., none of the students wants to be nominated, stand or vote? I found myself in this situation after accepting the task of entertainment co-ordinator. I called a meeting of the students. I explained that in my opinion entertainment was their business and I would act as co-ordinator only. I suggested that various tasks were to be carried out by students. Everybody agreed. I wrote all the different tasks to be performed on the blackboard and I proposed an election. Silence. I then explained that certain students might like to propose others for the job. Still silence. I then asked who would like to do one of the jobs. Dead silence. If I would suggest names of possible candidates would they vote for them? Still nothing. I took me two Saturday mornings to find out that in the students' opinion it was up to the teacher to nominate a student for a certain task. I refused and the compromise was that the students themselves would nominate a fellow student for a certain job. It was impossible for me to bring them to vote – to practise a democratic right – or even demonstrate openly their personal preferences. I have been thinking about it and have come to a number of conclusions. One of them is that you have to learn democracy and that the primary and secondary teachers in Lesotho I have met are not teaching democracy at all. Teaching on the whole in Lesotho is pretty authoritarian and learning by rote is common.

I once visited a primary school and all the pupils, aged from six till fifteen, were outside; I would think all in all a group of about a hundred pupils. They walked around alternatively touching a hand and their head, while saying in a monotonous drone, 'This is my hand and this is my head, this is my hand and this is my head'. When I asked my colleague to translate my question, 'What is this', while touching a pupil's head, none of them knew.

Most of the rural primary and secondary schools are rather badly off at the moment: no facilities, overcrowded classes, unqualified personnel, and so on. This situation causes the Ministry of Education great concern. At the moment the National Teacher Training Centre is being upgraded in a much-needed effort to improve the quality of their graduates.

For obvious reasons the few city schools are notably better and one of my early didactic problems was to assess the level of the students and subsequently try to form a more homogeneous group of students. Apart from big differences in English and science, there are tremendous variations in what the students know about agriculture. City dwelling students know almost as much about agriculture as any urbanite in Europe – practically nothing. For some reason I had always assumed that all African students would know quite a lot about agriculture in their own country. Not so in Lesotho, anyway. It turned out to be a sort of a equilibrium: those who were poor in English and science knew something about farming and those without the slightest idea about agriculture would be rather good in the other subjects. After forming, or at least trying to form, a more homogeneous group, I was confronted with the next problem: what should I teach?

The question was mine to answer because I had been asked to write the syllabus for extension education. The challenge was clear, but it was obvious from the start that I would run into problems with the main branch of the college by making extension one of the major subjects. I am convinced that at the moment the training offered at Leribe is substantially better than at Maseru, and the facts prove me right. Fortunately I have never felt seriously hampered by the lack of co-operation or even the more or less concealed hostility of the main branch. Much more irritating was, I found, having to write the syllabus without the help of a counterpart. Only long after the course had taken shape was my counterpart stationed at Leribe, and then only minor changes were possible. I am glad, though, that he did not want to make any major alternations.

Fortunately we are able to work together well. We visit each other's homes, discussing work and all aspects of life rather openly. One significant problem I found with most of my colleagues and all students is that they do not see farming as an extremely complex set of factors. They consistently try to isolate one of these interrelating factors. How many times have I heard statements like 'if only we could improve our livestock, we could save the nation'. It is very difficult to teach the students the connection between the different aspects of farming. This is mirrored in their enthusiastic and ambitious plans to lift one aspect of farming out of its context, see what is wrong with it, try to change it and expect miracles, for example by adopting the maxim 'dipping your sheep gives quick returns'.

I found it especially difficult to discuss these matters with students. They have never learnt to discuss and they are reluctant to express their ideas. I managed to still some of their fears through role plays. Playing the role of a farmer, a chief or an extension assistant helps the students to get over their shyness and, moreover, they are very keen to evaluate the plays afterwards. Still, the step from this evaluation to a more general group discussion is rather big. Nevertheless, the students become freer and on one occasion they even got enough courage together to question one aspect of my teaching: they found that they did not write enough.

I had noticed that some of my local colleagues would dictate their lectures for fifty minutes solid. The students claimed they learned very much. In my teaching, however, I write the outline on a flip-chart, put some words on the blackboard and all in all the students are able to take these notes within ten minutes per period. However, they claim they do not learn very much this way. I consider it a very delicate matter to discuss the teaching techniques of my colleagues with students. In very general terms I checked if they understood everything they had written down so devoutly and if they could explain all that information to others, which is after all the objective of extension training. To cut a long story short, they hardly understood the information given to them and in no way they could explain it to others. During a teachers' meeting I mentioned that some of the students had not completely understood some aspects of their training. Of course I did this in the most general terms. I am afraid that it served only to illustrate 'how stupid some of the students are.' Only with my own counterpart and one other colleague did I achieve some success. They introduced a short evaluation and revision into their teaching programme.

To a certain extent this is understandable as none of my colleagues are trained teachers. This combined with the fact that the students hardly ever ask questions, makes it very hard to assess with any degree of accuracy how well your audience understands you. Only a few weeks ago I was confronted by this while teaching a new group of first year students. I asked, 'Do you have any questions?' No answer. 'Did you all understand it?' Nothing. 'Who did understand it, please?' Still no reaction. 'Who did not understand it?' Still no reply. I carefully explained that it was impossible to have no answer on both of these questions, to which there was no reaction, not even hilarity; I just started asking questions on the substance of my talk to evaluate myself.

Hilarity. How important that can be. Nothing feels worse than to crack a joke during classes without getting any reaction. It feels especially bad when the students do not understand the joke and your whole motivation was based on it. It did teach me to improvise, though, in particular on how to motivate students. Stimuli that work rather well in the Netherlands do not necessarily appeal in Lesotho. I found that stimulating motives geared to avoiding painful situations work reasonably well. For instance, when I want to motivate students to use coloured chalk on the blackboard, they are much more impressed by the fact that if they do not use it people might think that they do not know how to use coloured chalk, rather than by the positive motivation that coloured chalk improves the blackboard layout and therefore makes the subject matter easier to understand. In general the students are very conscious of their impact on people. Even more so than in Europe, one should never ridicule a student in public.

I continue to be staggered by the lack of positive motivation of our students. They are very unknowing of their probable future and therefore uncertain and unable to take initiatives. I once experienced a striking example of this with a group of second year students. I cannot remember how we came to talk about it, but suddenly it dawned on me that none of these students knew what their future wages were going to be! They had never been told what their salary would be and they had never bothered to ask . . .

I am afraid that this behaviour of the students is being reinforced by the local staff. They even sometimes refer to the students as 'children'; they never encourage initiatives taken by the students and in general treat them as minors.

I tried during talks with colleagues to explain that in my opinion the lack of trust and the almost complete denial of students' responsibility has contributed to the failure of previous graduates. These graduates had to change from one day to the other from infantile students to responsible members of their society. No wonder many could not cope and tried to salve this harsh change with alcohol.

It makes me so angry to hear the director welcome new students with an hour-long speech filled to the brim with doom and gloom. 'If you don't work day and night, you will be expelled; if you don't study constantly you will be sorry you ever came here; if you don't work incessantly in your garden plot we will have to inform your parents that you are a complete failure.' When I was asked to 'warn' the students what to expect in extension training I tried to convey a feeling of them being welcome, a hope that they would enjoy their two-year stay, and the expectation that they would make good friends. Admittedly the director expressed his gratitude for my pep talk later, but still why scare the living daylights out of the students in the first place? Especially since he knows that the checking up on all the rules and regulations slackens within a couple of weeks to an almost unacceptably low level. I find it difficult to tread the middle path here.

In this respect it is worthwhile mentioning my problems in explaining to colleagues and students why a teacher should test his students. In the students' opinion a test is a punishment. Some admitted after discussion that a test could be used to assess how well they had studied, but the concept that a teacher should evaluate himself is alien to their thinking. I had to fight to get not only repetition of slogans tested during examinations, but also skills, attitudes and understanding. It is assumed by my local colleagues that as long as a student can repeat a phrase they automatically understand it. The gap between repetition and the desirable knowledge, skill and attitudes of an extension assistant is not or hardly felt.

For the past twenty-six years the Lesotho Agricultural College has been training young people to become extension assistants. Especially in the last couple of years it has become apparent that the present training is not suited to the job. Many graduates do not even join the Ministry of Agriculture but go straight across the border to South Africa to seek better paid employment in the mines. The quality of those who are employed by the Ministry is not always impressive. It came to me as a rather bad shock to find that the College has never undertaken an evaluation of their training.

WILLEM'S FLYING EXTENSION CIRCUS

I have a few comments on audio-visual aids. Shortly after my arrival at the Farmers Training Centre I was appointed, among other things, farm manager. Going through all the stores I found in one leaking shed with an earthen floor and no proper windows a sixteen millimetre sound projector, a portable tape recorder, two slide projectors, two typewriters and a film screen – this in addition to the four motor-driven lawn-mowers and other equipment. I could easily repair the slide projectors and the typewriters only needed new ribbons. The screens were perfect after a good wash, but the sound projector and the tape recorder missed essential parts that had been sent to the capital for repairs long before. Nobody knew where the parts were anymore, so unfortunately these machines were beyond repair. Then and there I decided not to use any electrical, complicated audio-visual aids in my talks, nor to teach anything about them to students, who in their work would not have electricity available anyway. Two ways to overcome the lack of fancy electrical gimmicks is, first, to go for reality and, second, to build or make your own aids. As far as reality is concerned the students go into the nearby villages one day per week. In addition they go into the field on different assignments during their holidays. No slide series or film show can compete with face-to-face contacts with the local farmers. Sometimes they are even coached on the spot by an experienced extension assistant.

Making your own aids can be fun too. I made with the students what we called Willem's Flying Extension Circus: two sheets of hardboard loosely connected at the top. One side is painted white – your filmscreen – another is painted black – that is the blackboard. On another side you glue flanel to make a flanelboard and on the fourth side you bolt on a pad for flip-charts. So far it has been pretty effective and the students seem to like it.

On two different occasions I witnessed something that strengthened my opinion not to use any sophisticated aids. I was asked to organize a course on the use of the overhead projector for the Farmer Training Centres' staff. Upon arrival at one of these centres I was confronted with a big box. 'This is the overhead projector, sir', they said. 'It arrived a couple of months ago'. They had not even bothered to open the box. Maybe they were just afraid to damage anything. On the second occasion I met an agricultural information service unit in the field. While they were getting out of the Landrover an expensive camera fell out on the rocky ground. When I glanced inside I saw a 16 mm sound projector lying loose in the back. There was no padding, no restraining ropes, or anything, and they had covered a rather rough track.

Things are slow to change they say. We are very far from our goal, indeed. But we are working at it. I feel that local and expatriate staff should try and work out a viable compromise to train our students in the best way. Nevertheless I should never forget that I am working in this country for many reasons. One is that I feel poor countries should develop themselves at a faster rate than they do and that therefore some outside help is needed. I hope I can provide some of that help. The local staff, however, does not necessarily have these underlying motives; for many of them it is just a job. Perhaps it is one of the most important aspects of an expatriate expert's work to motivate and stimulate his or her counterpart, to instill in them the feeling of pride in a job well done.

9 ABOUT SOIL CONSERVATION, TRAINING AND PEJORATIVES

Piet van der Poel

THE SETTING

The post of soil conservation officer that I held in Botswana is not primarily a teaching job, but includes, in addition to organizational and administrative duties, on-the-job training and short courses for the soil-conservation staff. I will deal with problems encountered in these aspects of my work, as well as with those specifically concerned with having a job within the system of government of Botswana.

Botswana is a country in southern Africa with about one million inhabitants. Cattle used to be the main source of income, but recently mining and processing of diamonds have become more important. Agriculture is mainly practised on a subsistance level. Soil conservation problems are minor compared to other African countries (for example, Lesotho).

The Ministry of Agriculture in Gaborone is housed in five blocks of long, wooden buildings and, since recently, a two-story, red brick, main building. The ministry is organized in departments. These are subdivided into divisions, which are subdivided into sections. The soil conservation section belongs to the land utilization division, which is part of the field services department. The minister is assisted by a permanent secretary, a deputy permanent secretary and others. Each department has its director, each division its chief and each section its head.

THE PLAYERS

I will briefly introduce a number of people that I mention in this account of my first experiences as a development worker in Botswana.

Mr Masete was the senior agricultural and live-stock officer at soil conservation when I arrived. He is a friendly man who was unfortunately promoted into the wrong section, as he happened to know less about soil conservation than his assistants. He retired in April 1979 to start a flourishing butchery.

His replacement was Moses, a tall young fellow with a diploma in agriculture and some training in land-use planning. Prior to joining the section he had a position as assistant agricultural officer land resources.

Mphathi is the man who ran the soil conservation section before my arrival. He had left to study in the USA and would, I was told, upon his return take

100

over as soil conservation officer. He returned in May 1980 and took over the post of land development officer. Soil conservation was one of his responsibilities.

The soil conservation section has assistants stationed throughout the country. The ones I worked with at various locations were Donald, Japie, Mpe, Pax, Moagi, Ben, Ocean, Bucs, Calvin and Jomo & Co. The last person to mention is Piet, a soil conservation officer, Dutch FAO associate-expert and geomorphologist with two years previous experience in Somalia. He was not very familiar with the engineering aspects of soil conservation, though. Later on he worked on a direct contract with the government of Botswana for about six months.

The main task for the section is to prevent or stop erosion of arable land by convincing farmers to use conservation methods and build structures that will stop erosion. Each district is supposed to have its own soil conservation assistant. Furthermore there is a small research program to collect data on rainfall erosivity, runoff and soil loss and a sand-dune stabilization project at Bokspits in southwest Botswana in the Kalahari Desert. The soil conservation officer is responsible for running, organizing and administrating the section. He also visits the assistants to check their work and organizes two soil conservation courses per year: one week for the new assistants and the trained field assistants, and the second week for all soil conservation assistants.

BUREAUCRACY AND BUDGETING

Like any bureaucratic organization the Botswana Government has piles of rules and regulations. As I had been initially employed by an even more bureaucratic organization, the Food and Agricultural Organization of the United Nations, and after two years was still trying to learn their rules and regulations, I did not try very hard to get familiar with all the rules and regulations of the Botswana Government and the Ministry of Agriculture that concerned me or the assistants. Besides, I am not very fond of working through piles of paper just to find the few rules and regulations applicable to my situation. Consequently whenever assistants or field assistants enquired about their travel allowance, promotion, bicycle allowance, etc., I had to tell them that I would check on it or, as in most cases, I would ask Mr Masete or Moses to check on it for them. This caused considerable delay and uneasiness among the assistants as it often took a month before a reply reached them.

When I was briefed about the job I was told that I should work in the soil conservation section together with Mr Masete, but I was not told whether I was in a higher position or not. The assistants were not sure of my position either; some of them thought I was some volunteer and as such was definitely not in charge of the section, and consequently not their superior. This meant I could not just tell an assistant to keep quiet, while later Moses could say the same things without problems.

The financial system of the government of Botswana is somewhat flexible. Within a financial year money for specific purchases is allocated through specific

votes. But this money does not necessarily have to be spent on those items. Other items falling within the same category could be purchased instead. The amounts, however, are limited and once the money in a particular vote is spent it is difficult to get more. I had problems with my budgets, primarily because I had to work with budgets I never drew up. During the nine months of my first year in the section I had to work with a budget drawn up by the land development officer. The year after that my budget was mainly drawn up by Mr Masete, as I was still orienting myself at the time. The biggest problems arose with the sand-dune stabilization project, for which only 300 Pula[1] was available in our budget. This happened to be about 800 Pula short of the amount needed for only fencing the five hectare plot. This extra money could quite easily be obtained from the Agricultural Resources Board, a body that allocates money to reclamation projects. The next problem was that no money was available for watering equipment, needed to water the tree seedlings to be planted. But at the end of the financial year other sections or departments often have money left in their votes and this can, with the usual amount of paper work, be transferred to other sections. This way I was able to buy water drums, hose-pipes, buckets and two donkeys, harnesses and a donkey cart for transporting water.

Overgrazing in and around Bokspits is so severe that most of the year no fodder is available. Consequently, additional fodder has to be brought in. During my first year this could be obtained from different departments of the ministry. After the usual frustrations of organizing transport (the soil conservation section does not have a five-ton truck of its own) the fodder was delivered to Bokspits. In the 1980–1981 budget I had money to extend the water pipeline of the district council into the plot, but permission to do so was only received in June 1980, and then only after much pressure had been applied. I had hoped to have the pipeline constructed in April 1980 and to get rid of the donkeys at the same time, so I had not requested any money for additional fodder. But at that time, at the beginning of the financial year, none of the other departments could provide me with any money, and the donkeys were starving by the time the pipeline was finished.

In the 1980–1981 budget about three quarters the amounts I submitted were cut. The land development officer finally obtained money for the research programme but this caused six months delay. Because of this delay I was not able to get the runoff and soil-loss measurement programmes into full operation by the time I left Botswana. Such financial arrangements take a lot of time because all sorts of official letters have to be written before money can be transferred. Especially in the beginning, when I was not familiar with the correct ways of dealing with these problems, I found it a very frustrating experience, although in the end I often succeeded in getting the money I needed.

---

1   US $1.00 = 0.83 Pula.

CAN I BORROW YOUR LANDROVER?

One of the biggest problems in the section is transport – the unreliability and lack of it. The assistants stationed out of Gaborone had to be visited once a month, mostly for one day. Those stationed in Gaborone were seen more regularly, often for shorter periods, although more time was spent with the less-experienced assistants.

It is almost impossible to work without transport. Soil conservation assistants work in different villages in their districts, and carry with them survey equipment, maps, camping equipment, etc. On my arrival the section had two vehicles for nine officers and assistants. The UN provided me with a very unreliable Landrover, which ran off the road six times because of mechanical defects. Later on we received one additional vehicle. Still this was very insufficient, especially because most of the cars were old and I often had to run around to try to borrow vehicles from other officers. Problems get even worse when borrowed vehicles break down or overturn and are under repair for weeks. In such cases I also had to provide the person who lent the vehicle with transport. I have had quite some frustrating hours trying to arrange transport.

My worst experience was the time when I came back from a one-week visit to assistants in Tati, Tukume and Motshegaletau, and hoped, after I found our own vehicle still awaiting vital spare parts, to be allowed to use the same borrowed vehicle I had been using the next day to go on a eight-day trip to the sand-dune stabilization project in Bokspits. As the chief who had lent me the vehicle was absent on my return, I loaded it with hay. When I arrived next morning I learnt that the chief did not want to lend me the vehicle any longer, although he did not need it himself. After hours of running around trying to find other cars I was told by the land development officer that the chief wanted the vehicle back immediately. I had to go back to unload the hay, only to be fined on the way for speeding. When I returned the keys I heard that I could keep the car. By then I had lost four hours and sixty Pula for the fine. I felt like being really rude to the chief, but I just smiled, thanked him and went back to reload the hay, this time avoiding the speed-trap.

It is possible, but time-consuming, to construct conservation banks with simple equipment such as the Morris ditcher, which can be drawn by a tractor, oxen or donkeys. But for storm-water drains or waterways heavier equipment is needed. All heavy equipment of the soil conservation section, apart from one tractor, is borrowed from the forestry section or the agricultural resources board. This includes a tractor, two towed graders, a subsoiler and a water bowser, which have been lent out on a permanent basis. Other equipment has to be borrowed from other sections or the agricultural research station. Funds for purchasing our own equipment as submitted in the 1980–1981 budget were not allocated, so the time-consuming and plan-upsetting business of borrowing had to continue. However, in the end you become an expert in knowing where to borrow what.

104

'YOU DO IT YOURSELF'

Initial social problems with the soil conservation assistants were at least partly due to the fact that the working relationship between the land development officer, nicknamed Rra Boloto ('Mr Graded Bank'), and the assistants was somewhat strained. I was immediately classified as one of his men and consequently treated as such. Besides, the assistants were not sure of my position within the section and some thought that I was definitely not their superior.

Cultural differences of which I was not aware, such as the use of certain pejoratives, also led to problems with the assistants. Once when I told Mpe, Ben and Calvin that they were talking 'bullshit', they did not say I should not use that word but instead they said that I had insulted them. In reaction Mpe later told me that all of us whites were just there to suppress them. Then I felt insulted.

The tense atmosphere between the assistants and me showed itself another time, when during the agricultural show Male was driving at about fifty kilometres per hour at the show-ground, where a lot of people were walking; the speedlimit was fifteen kilometres per hour. When I asked and then had to tell him to drive slower he became angry. He argued that he was the driver and knew how to drive and if I knew better I could drive. So he stopped and got out the vehicle. I had to ask him to get back in and drive back to the office, which he finally did. Japie later told me I was completely right – some support I badly needed.

Problems with Mpe continued for a long while, until at a certain point in time I gave up arguing with him and just told him what I wanted him to do and ignored his usual 'you do it yourself' and 'that is none of my business'. Although this is not the way I like to work, it was effective and not so frustrating. Mr Masete was not of much help because he did not spend much time in the field, because of his limited technical knowledge. The situation improved slowly, especially after Moses joined the soil conservation section. He did not have the same expatriate-counterpart or white-black problems.

ABOUT LANGUAGE AND LUNCH TIME

Cultural differences are an unavoidable fact. I cannot deny my upbringing and cultural background. For instance, I normally prefer to eat with a fork instead of with my fingers, although I am prepared at any time to use my fingers. I am also prepared to eat local food: mealiemeal, tripe or goats feet. I think I am prepared to go a long way to try to adapt where necessary to local customs. In doing so I think I can be expected to make mistakes, too, but I should not be blamed for those I make unknowingly.

When I began with the section I was told that it would be better if the assistants stayed out in the field for lunch rather than loosing half the day by travelling back and forth to the worksite. When I proposed this once to Mpe, Calvin and Ben, they were working twelve kilometres from the office. I was told, mainly by Mpe, that it was impossible. They had to have their mealiemeal at lunch time and could not eat bread, so they could not take a packed lunch. I said that if I could eat mealiemeal I could not see why they could not eat bread. I refered to their argument as 'bullshit'. This changed the matter immediately: they accused me of insulting them. I had to talk for a long time to convince them – only partially – that I had not intended to insult them. A bit later when I used the word nonsense the same thing happened. I finally had to leave the subject alone, with them coming back for lunch, because they were mostly working on their own and I did not find the matter significant enough to create a bigger fuss over.

Something similar happened later with Moagi, who I had brought to a field where he was to work for some days. When I wanted to leave him there just before lunch time he insisted on me taking him twenty-five kilometres back to town and returning him in the afternoon, as he had no money to buy himself lunch. I offered to lend him money but he refused. Finally I left him behind. He was angry and I was not very happy with the 'solution', but I had to make him understand that I was not going to play taxi-driver.

All assistants speak English fairly well and a big part of their education was in English. I put in some effort to learn Setswana but I did not get much further than the basic greetings and some simple questions and answers. In my work and living situation Setswana was not necessary as everything could be done in English. My clashes with the assistants did not motivate me to put in much effort either. In the beginning when addressed in Setswana by the assistants, I used to answer in Somali (I had worked previously in Somalia), 'Ma agaan of Setswana' or, 'I don't know Setswana', which they understood as 'ke agana Setswana', meaning, 'I refuse Setswana'. Naturally they did not appreciate that. Another misunderstanding due to language arose because of the way Moagi asked things, saying 'why don't you do this', 'why don't you do that', which at first gave me the impression that he had a rather aggressive and violent character. It took me some time to find out that he really meant 'couldn't you do this', 'couldn't you do that'.

TRAINING BY TRIAL AND ERROR

I had enough theoretical background for my job, but I certainly needed a little more technical and practical knowledge and experience. It took me some months to get familiar with that aspect of the job. By watching the assistants working in the field, checking their maps and asking questions I got a reasonable idea of their knowledge. Calvin did not know at all how to use a dumpy level for surveying and none of the other assistants had bothered to explain it to him. At first I thought that Calvin was a field assistant. When I started to teach him how to survey he immediately became more friendly. I also found that some assistants did not want to admit their ignorance and were afraid to ask for help.

I once sent Ocean out to survey the boundaries of fifteen fields in Mookane. I spent one day with him, during which he surveyed and drew the map of the boundaries of the first field. I left thinking he knew what he was doing. When he returned to the office two weeks later he showed me his maps, but he had not brought his survey books, making checking of the maps impossible. He returned to Mookane to finish the rest of the fields. On his next return I found that most of his maps did not bear any relationship to the data in his survey books. Finally I understood that most of his directions were not right because most of the time he used his protractor wrongly and then adjusted his measurements to make them fit the survey readings. I spent another three days with him in the field checking his surveys. Although he half-heartedly denied that he had been cheating I convinced him that it would have been better if he had asked me earlier to help him.

Another problem is that a lot of mistakes made by the assistants during field-work cannot immediately be corrected. Ben had once constructed some graded banks wrongly. There were high and low spots in the channel that would cause the banks to break sooner or later. However equipment to adjust the mistake is never readily available. Consequently, I had to ask him to check all his banks and dig out the high spots and fill up the low ones. On my next visits he happened to be working in other areas 50 to 100 kilometres away and it took months before I had another opportunity to check that particular area.

Each year, around November, a two-week training course is organized. The first week, a basic course is attended by relatively new assistants, trained field assistants and some assistants from other land utilization sections. The second week of training is on a more advanced level and meant for all soil conservation assistants. About ten people attended each course. The *basic course* gave very few problems. I was familiar with almost all its aspects and knew that Jomo & Co were familiar with the actual construction of graded banks. This course was mainly practical, including surveying and mapping of boundaries and contours of a field, and the design, pegging out and construction of graded banks. I found that for most of the attendants the subject of designing graded banks was too difficult. Ben, Ocean and Bucs had to become familiar with the designing outside the course; for the others this task was still too complicated. However I did not take this aspect out of the course because it is part of a complete programme.

The main problems I met during this course were organizational: breakdown of the tractor forced us to postpone the construction; breakdown of two vehicles, which could luckily be replaced by 'borrowing' vehicles from the land development officer before he arrived at the office; and bad weather or muddy fields, which delayed field work. Another problem was that one particular practice field was too far away. By changing the timetable, however, we managed to stay most of the morning in the field; the drawing, designing and explanation was done in the afternoons.

There was always a good atmosphere on the course and the trainees showed a lot of interest. One year the Tuesday was suddenly declared an official holiday. I told the trainees that it was impossible to squeeze the programme into four days and that I was prepared to work that holiday, but if they wanted to celebrate the holiday they were free to do so. All but one of them turned up.

The first year I gave the course Moagi assisted me, the second year Moses and

Moagi and in the third year the course was given completely by Moses, Moagi and Mpe. This had the advantage, especially for the field assistants, who are less familiar with English, that things could be explained in Setswana.

The *more advanced course* gave more problems. The first year I decided to go through all aspects of soil conservation and emphasize the theoretical side of the subject, because I was at that time still not very familiar with the technical side and because there was a lack of time to prepare. Only a couple of weeks before the course started I was asked by the land development officer to check with the rural training centre if any course was booked. I knew that the older assistants had dealt with quite a number of the theoretical aspects of soil conservation during an earlier course and accepted that for them part of the course should serve to refresh their knowledge. The main complaint was that the course was too much of 'the old stuff' and that it should contain more practical work.

The following years I asked the assistants which aspects they wanted me to teach during the course. Bucs was about the only one to give suggestions, but I knew that some of them were not at all acceptable to the older assistants. So I invited more guest speakers and selected a number of special items to deal with in more detail. Most of these items included practical work. Again there were complaints about covering things the assistants 'knew' already. This often meant that they had been told about the subject before, but they had never tried to put it into practice.

The diversity within the group of soil conservation assistants makes it impossible to organize a course that satisfies everybody. Donald often complained that I was confusing him: he had learned a method of designing banks by trial and error, which every now and then led him to comment that at a certain place no graded bank could be designed. A general problem with most assistants is the very low level of their mathematics. Mpe argued that some of the practical work was below his level and he preferred to learn how to construct gully-control structures, which meant that he watched everybody else doing the work. The practical designing exercise was a big problem as I was not able to check all nine assistants, in particular because the less experienced assistants needed quite some attention.

I see that I have painted a picture that is one-sidedly gloomy, yet there were enough positive experiences to keep me going. In and around the office things usually went well. Most of my negative experiences occurred in the beginning, and then while I was working in the field or outside working hours.

10 YOU REALLY ARE A CHILD

Theo Groot

FROM POLDER TO RAIN FOREST

In May 1979, after having finished my training at the Hogere Landbouw-school (School for Higher Agricultural Education) in Dronten, the Netherlands, I left as a development volunteer for Basankusu in Zaire. Here I work in the service of the diocese. In the heart of this equatorial rain forest, together with others, I am trying to help bring about rural development. It is rather difficult and every now and again I ask myself what is the use of it all. And yet it is precisely this challenging situation that makes it so interesting. Little by little we have to find our way.

First of all we try to formulate a sort of development policy: what are the possibilities in this area for the promotion of rural development and what obstacles will we meet as we try to realize them. All the time we try to integrate theory and practice.

Another important aspect of our work concerns the education of local people. We do this in three different ways. First of all, we have the training centre for Zairian brothers[1]. They will work as rural development workers after their training. Besides the centre we have also started a course in agriculture for people of the village. We discuss agriculture and rural development with the villagers and we try to realize something of our development policy. Finally, I have started to train two local teachers to be my assistants.

These experiences and the talks I have had with people on this subject are the basis for my story. It is just a collection of personal impressions and thoughts – 'snapshots'. It is by no means intended as a general statement.

CHANGE IN SOCIAL POSITION

A society is a living community of people. It is not at all uniform and equal, neither in Europe nor in Africa. It is a composite of social ranks, and as a

---

1 These brothers are members of the religious brother congregation 'Balangwa Kristu', founded by the local bishop in 1977. They have dedicated their lives to village development in the poor rural areas of Zaire.

volunteer you have to be very well aware of this social hierarchy and of your place in it. Your position in the 'field' may very well differ from your position in Europe. In Europe a strong relation exists between social and economic position. Someone who has a lot of money and possessions is a rich man from an economic point of view. He occupies a high place on the social ladder; wealth is equal to influence and power. Most of you, that is to say the people to whom this essay refers, have just finished your studies or training. You have no, or hardly any, teaching experience in Europe. In Holland you had a *'students position'*, both socially and economically. But when you arrive in a developing country this position changes too. You will occupy a higher position on the social ladder and in the given local situation you may even reach the top of that ladder. Did you once belong to the 'have-less'; there you belong to the elite, notwithstanding your simple life-style. I will discuss the problems raised by this drastic change in economic position further on. First I will go a little further into the social aspects of this change.

The natural relationship that exists in Europe between someone's bank account and his 'standing' is less common in Zaire. Here place in society is strongly defined by age. The *nkumu*[1] in a village is someone who has been chosen for his age and the magical powers people attribute to him. When this person is also economically wealthy it is because of his being nkumu and not the other way around. But money does play a much bigger role nowadays. This means that personal esteem may also be determined by financial position. A rich person is called *mokonzi,* but the power he possesses is only economical. Federal officers and politicians are also mokonzi because of their political power. A mokonzi is someone who for economic or political reasons can impose his power.

What does this all have to do with my work in the village? Upon my arrival I immediately joined the economic elite. I became mokonzi, but socially I am – because of my age – regarded as a child. If you are in the service of a school this may be less strong, but here in the villages I have heard more than once *yo ozali mwana mpenza* ('you really are a child'). It is from this position that I have to talk with people about village development. If I keep this idea strongly in mind, people will pay attention to what I say. But if I impose myself upon them as the 'agricultural expert', people will listen politely and give me the impression that I am indeed the expert – but that's all.

BEING WHITE

Apart from my social and economic position, the colour of my skin also influences the expectations people have of me. First of all, white is considered equal to honest and just. In a country that is corrupt from top to bottom and

---

1   The word 'nkumu' can be translated by 'elders'. It refers to the traditional chiefs of the clan and the village. The word 'mokonzi' on the other hand refers to people having a certain influence on account of their political or economic position in modern society. It can be translated by our word 'lord'.

where hardly anyone can be trusted, you enjoy an almost fabulous confidence as far as money is concerned.

White is also being looked upon as better. Goods from Europe are for that very reason automatically better. A clinic with a white nurse is evidently better and if teachers of the nearby secondary school urge me to come and teach there it is mainly for that same reason. It is taken for granted that white teachers are better than black ones, although experience proves that this is not always true. Another example I can give in this context concerns an annual report of the local authorities. After they described the miserable situation with regard to the rural development they drew but one conclusion: 'de trouver un responsable blanc'.

These attitudes are deeply rooted in an inferiority complex of the people. This is proved by the fact that every affirmation of self-respect and encouragement to be honest and dedicated is answered with the remark *'yo ozali modele, kasi biso moindo tokoki kosala boye te'* ('you are white, but we black people are not able to do so'). This feeling of inferiority is a serious problem in direct communication with villagers. The only solution is to give a good example and to convince people of their potential, to help them rediscover their self-respect.

BEING LONELY

Once I had settled in a bit and found my way, I was confronted with another problem, that of loneliness. In Europe there was an overwhelming amount of information and I had very many contacts. I could always talk about my problems with someone and life offered enough distractions. Here I am rather isolated. There are only a few contacts so that I am completely thrown back upon myself. I have not chosen the people with whom I live and work but I am 'condemned' to share my life with them. It is not easy to make contacts with the local population, especially in the beginning. And when I am approached it is often more because of what I have than who I am.

In Europe there is a fairly one-sided view of the African situation. Rightly, the structural inequality of their development is stressed very much. The image we get of the African is that of an exploited and oppressed human being, attempting to take the development of his country and life in his own hands. This may sound a bit like an exaggeration but I think it is not so far from the truth. To me it was quite an experience to find out that people here are – not unlike ourselves – made of flesh and blood, with their good and their bad qualities. It is painful to see that the causes for underdevelopment are not only external, but that there are also internal, human, obstacles to their own development.

This experience forced me to face the truth, to discard the one-sided European view. Through all this I experienced feelings of loneliness, desperation and doubt. It is a very enriching experience, however, if you are able to keep an 'open mind', if you dare to descend into your deepest self and face all these questions. Defining a right attitude towards this situation is crucial for the continuation of your contract period. However, too often this crisis impoverishes a person instead of enriching him. It can lead to a bitter attitude towards the population,

112

to escape in liquor and sex, to the formation of a white clique, to seclusion and isolation.

BEING RICH

As I have already said, as soon as I arrived in Basangkusu I immediately joined the economic top-layer of society. In one day I exchanged my simple student's position for that of a rich person. The gap between rich and poor, which is discussed infinitely in Europe, presented itself very clearly to me. It is a gap between me and the others.

One of the first expressions I learned in Lingala[1] was *pesa ngai* ('give me'), which is followed by a list varying from clothes, to shoes, exercise books, food, money and so on. Some people fire these questions at you without any diplomacy, others tell an introductory story more than an hour long. Your first impression is: 'How nice, they came along for a chat'. But finally they as well turn up with the same question 'pesa ngai'. And if you do not meet their wishes, like some Father Christmas, there is but one conclusion for the asker: he is not willing to give me something; he can afford it but he is just not willing. The confrontation is there, you cannot avoid it. There are big economic differences between you and the people around you, your colleagues and the people in the villages. This is a painful situation and it always results in confrontation. Someone who no longer experiences this as painful is already too much of an 'old hand'.

CULTURAL CHANGE

The confrontation with another culture made me aware of my own cultural background. It was an enriching experience to discover that the values we Europeans cling to do not have the same meaning in a different cultural context. To us it is a matter of politeness to say 'thank you' whenever someone has given something to you. Here people accept things in a slightly different manner. They seem to think 'you just did what you had to do'. When we see someone trying hard to get something done, we consider it normal to give him a hand. Here crowds can stand around you, watching how desperately you are trying to manage for yourself.

But unfortunately there are still people who live two years or more in Africa without changing at all. They only get angry when confronted with different attitudes towards their 'holy' values. You need – I think – a bit of an anthropological attitude. Because if you do not dare to throw yourself into daily life, if you prefer for example to stay in the school compound, you will never have the

---

1   Lingala is the inter-tribal language that is spoken in a great part of Zaire. Its role may be compared to that of Swahili in East Africa.

slightest notion of what is going on in that fascinating world around you. Knowing the language is one of the first steps on the way. Apart from the official language, you should also learn, or at least make an effort to learn, a bit of the local language. The mere attempt breaks down a tremendous barrier between you and the local people, for it is a sign of your interest in them.

CONCEPT OF TIME

In this age of discoveries the question arises whether or not people really are so lazy as evil tongues would have us believe. A first look could indeed give that impression. In the beginning I ascribed the people's lack of enthousiasm and dedication to the climate and fatalism, but I discovered soon enough that it is at best only part of the truth. The problem lies much deeper and has to do with their concept of time.

To me, from a Western, technical, society, time is economically determined. Time is a commodity to be utilized, sold and bought. Time is money. But in traditional African life, time has to be created or produced. Man is not a slave of time, instead he 'makes' as much time as he wants. When we see people sitting down somewhere, obviously doing nothing, we tend to say 'they waste their time by just sitting there'. However this judgement is based on ignorance of what time means to African people. Those who are sitting down are actually not wasting their time but rather they are either waiting for time or in the process of 'producing' time. For them time is two dimensional: it includes a long past, a present and hardly any future. This absence of a future perspective might be one of the reasons for what we define as 'an incomprehensible lack of planning'.

CONCEPT OF WRONG

He used to drop in regularly, Salazar, a guy of about twenty years of age. We chatted a bit about all kind of things and one day we came to talk about growing peanuts. The price on the market was extremely high and therefore he had the idea to start a field with peanuts. He turned me inside out with questions on this subject. Of course I answered with wholehearted enthusiasm. The village he lived in was about twenty kilometres away. Since I had no transport and was not that keen to go there on foot, I didn't have a chance to go and have a look. However according to his reports the work was advancing steadily. One day the field was prepared and the seeds could be sown. But there was a small problem. Salazar did not have enough money to buy the seeds he needed. Couldn't I lend him some? The little warning voice inside me was told to shut up – nothing ventured, nothing gained – and I gave him the money needed. Very happily he went home. I did not see him for a month, and then just a few days before I was intending to go and see what was happening, I met him again. The peanuts were growing fine. 'Well that is great,' I said, 'next week I'm coming along to have a look'. And with a still smiling face he told me that I would be very welcome. Imagine my amazement when upon my arrival I found but a few square metres of ground, obviously cleaned at the top of ones speed, with a few peanuts waiting for the first rains to come. The list of excuses seemed endless, but one thing was clear, it was not his fault. I really was disillusioned, not because Salazar had deceived me but because of the way he did it. I could not stand the abominable hypocrisy faced out to the last.

This is something I noticed several times afterwards. I think this kind of hypocrisy, at least this is the way I see it, has everything to do with your own conception of fault, doing wrong, badness, mistakes, etc. Only if the result of a certain action is wrong or bad is the deed itself considered bad, and even then people will try to prove that the real cause is beyond them. 'I did not steal, my hand just took something'. If a certain action has no bad consequences, then the deed is not bad either, which means that as long as a certain act stays unknown or hidden, insincerity and wickedness is out of the question. Salazar did no wrong at all, on the contrary, he was a clever guy who was just not very lucky.

CONCEPT OF RESPONSIBILITY

The road between Abunakombo and Basankusu has been since January 1980 impassable, and if all the time that has been used talking about it had been used to do something about it, we would be a long way towards fixing it already. Recently quite some money was collected to improve the road. Up till now not much has changed, but most of the money has disappeared, or as they say here, has been misplaced.

I really wonder if the responsible officials do not feel uncomfortable at least, because the beautiful titles they carry (of which they are very proud) in no way match their deeds. In Holland a person is what he does, and the 'doing' is economically measured. Someone who does not produce is no-one; he does not count. In Zaire we seem to fall into the other extreme. People are more important because of the title they carry. What they actually do is less important. And it is not too difficult to get a title. They can be bought, or even stolen.

A teacher will proudly tell you that he is a teacher. That he is sometimes useless at his job does not matter. His honor lies in his title and not in the results gained by his pupils. Teachers always have very many excuses for their professional shortcomings: no transport, not being paid, no books, no food, no this, no that. Most of the time they are right, but it makes me wonder, and it also hampers co-operation with my local colleagues. I regret that very much.

CONCEPT OF LOGIC

It was on a Friday evening that Songolo came along for a chat. He had a sore arm and my suggestion that he had probably a strained muscle was immediately put aside. It was something much more serious, this sickness was called *mopanzi*[1]. Someone had sent him a *ndoki*, a bad spirit; a salve would not do any good. This kind of disease needed a special kind of treatment. He had already been to a witchdoctor and he showed me the hair of an elephant's tail he wore around his wrist. He told me a lot of other stories and events to prove the existance of ndokis and other supernatural forces. One of the stories concerned the girl that was staying at his house. She was used by her ancestors as a medium to contact the living. She could go into a trance and a deceased could then talk through her. For me it was a strange, mysterious evening, especially because Songolo is rather educated and acquainted with modern ideas. Nevertheless he seemed to be absolutely convinced. There was more to come, for a few days later, early in the evening, a young man came to collect me. 'Songolo asks you to come to his house', he said. When I arrived the seance had just started. The girl he had talked about was crawling on the floor and she shivered all over her body, producing incomprehensible sounds. Besides Songolo there were one or two students present who lived in that same house. After a few minutes she calmed down, but all of a sudden it started again and so it went on for an hour-and-a-half. Then she started singing with a clear voice and all those present repeated the same words. She started talking, first murmuring but soon the words could be understood. Songolo told me that it was his late grandfather who spoke to us through her. He confirmed his ill-health being a real 'mopanzi'. He had probably asked for a bit of *lotoko*[2], for someone went to get some. When he came back, he put the bottle with a glass in front of the girl and although she shivered tremendously, she poured out a glass with a firm hand. She took a sip, passed the glass to Songolo who finished it, then she poured out another one and sprinkled it on the floor. The grandfather left, and while she was there, shivering and shaking very much, another person entered into her. It appeared to be a real witchdoctor from a nearby village who had died four days ago. On his command one of the boys went outside with a lamp to gather some weeds. The girl took them and she started to massage and to stroke Songolo's arm with the weeds. He was sitting in front of the girl, bare-chested. It took about ten minutes, then she shuffled to the far end of the room, sat quietly for a few minutes, stood up and went to wash herself as if nothing had happened. The boys went to bed. Songolo told me the pain had gone and he felt fine now. A bit perplexed, I went home.

Events like this are very common. Superstition, occultism and spirits are a real part of life in Basankusu. Healing as I have described above is just as logical as a treatment in the dispensary. For some diseases you have to see the nurse, for others, like mopanzi, you have to see the witchdoctor. We are apt to say that

1 'Mopanzi' is a state of ill-health caused by evil spirits, sent to you by some other person. This person may put *nkisi* (traditional medicine) on the road and when you pass you are 'infected' and you will get this mopanzi.
2 'Lotoko' is a local alcoholic drink that is distilled from a mixture of manioc and maize. It has an alcohol percentage of between 40 and 90%.

these people live in two worlds and that it is hard to understand how an educated man like Songolo still believes in these things. He is even convinced that men can change into elephants. When you start laughing about it, you risk that people will not tell you anything about it anymore, but if you take it seriously it makes you look at things in a different way. For is it not rather our logic that is not so logical?

We only perceive something in such a way that the object to know is in us. The supernatural world has been eliminated from our minds. Our perfect educational system has been teaching us that there is only one world with one kind of problems: the convergent ones, i.e. problems that can be analysed and solved scientifically. The problems that are not solved as yet will certainly be dealt with in the future. But what about these other kinds of problems, the divergent ones? What about questions like disease, suffering, death and life? Science cannot give an answer. Why has a mother of three little children to die because of cancer? Why has Alongea, one of the village women, to lose two children in one year? Here illhealth and death are signs of a disturbed relation, the cancer of that woman or the pneumonia of the children are the causes, but not the reasons, for their death.

To these people this is not strange at all. But we regard their solutions to these questions as being 'opium', primitive and underdeveloped. When you are confronted with these situations you may be confused, but if you keep an open mind and if you show your interest you might discover a mysterious world that makes you ask very many questions.

A SCHOOL AS A CENTRE OF (DE)FORMATION

Everyone with whom you talk and who is working in education in Zaire asks himself the same question: 'What is the use of this system of schooling'? What is the use of a system that alienates children from their home situation, that gives them false hopes, that makes them refuse to work with their hands? In short, a system that produces an immense proletariat of unsatisfied and disillusioned people. Of course this is not a problem specific to Zaire, one will probably find it all over Africa, and even in Europe. In Basankusu, however, the problem becomes manifest in its entirety. The school does not meet the real educational needs. It is not able to train people to take their own development in their own hands. It is deforming rather than forming.

That may be my opinion, but the problem is that my pupils, my colleagues and even the men at the top have other educational needs in mind: getting a white collar job, being someone with a big title, and so on. The common factor is that everybody wants to change their actual material situation. However, they prefer to escape this situation rather than to improve it. This explains the quick turnover of teachers in secondary schools. Almost every year the whole teaching staff is replaced by new people. In their turn, they will leave after one or two years, hoping to find a better position elsewhere, where they will be paid regularly, where they can earn their living a bit easier and where they will find less difficult working circumstances (enough books and chalk for instance).

If one cannot reach the top in a more or less legal way, one simply uses other means. One tampers with examination papers, one buys the desired certificate, or one simply steals it. It is a vicious circle and it takes an awful long time for people to realize that there is no way to escape by this system of schooling. The only solution is to join hands and to improve the actual situation.

This is one of the fundamental problems you have to deal with if you decide to teach. You should think twice, for it may be a very discouraging job, unless you just want to escape your own European situation for a while! But even then you need adaptability and the power to see things in a relative way.

TO TEACH OR TO LEARN

Fortunately the situation in which I am involved is slightly different, since I am an instructor for rural development workers rather than a teacher. As such, I have nothing to do with the official school, nevertheless I too am confronted with the low standards of my pupils.

One of the first problems to face is 'getting a thorough knowledge of the local situation'. Although my pupils are Zairians, this does not mean that they are aware of and acquainted with the problems and feelings of the people in the village. They too have to learn to see village life through the eyes of the villagers. It is difficult, however, to train them in this way and to design a programme that aims at real integration of theory and practice if you do not know what is going on at that same village level. To acquire at least a basic knowledge I would need more than a year-and-a-half, for in the beginning you are very handicapped because of the language problem. I regret it, but I could not spend such a length of time on nothing but this 'anthropological fieldwork', for I had to start the training courses. I had to develop a syllabus and define the objectives. It is just as challenging as it is frustrating when you always have to change, re-adapt, rewrite and sometimes redo. I was and still am in a constant process of growth.

Some time ago I was asked to give a basic course on agriculture and animal husbandry in our region[1]. I wanted to start with a small group of ten people in a nearby village. To select these ten people we asked all those interested to fill in an information sheet. We got about seventy applicants! All of them wanted to go to the *kelasi* ('school'). This is another problem with regard to rural development. Everyone is so obsessed by the idea of going to school and getting a diploma to leave or to escape that this becomes their main motivation. Time and again I have had to explain to people that I do not give a 'kelasi'. The aim is that they discuss together, learn together and work together to improve their own living conditions.

---

1   Our village development programme as well as the training courses for the brothers are based on the didactic material of INADES (Institut Africain pour le Développement Economique et Social) in Abidjan, Ivory Coast. In Zaire the material is circulated by CEPAS (Centre d'Etudes pour l'Action Social) in Kinshasa.

118

This 'kelasi' idea also influences the way in which the people on the course participate. They hardly understand that we want *participation au lieu d'encadrement*. To them to learn means to learn by heart. They will tell you they fully understand what you are saying, but what they mean is 'we can repeat it'. However it is doubtful whether they master the subject matter presented to them. Misapplication might well be caused by a lack of comprehension. I notice this very often when I ask someone to give a summary. It probably also has something to do with their concept of logic, for it is often very difficult for them to get to the point, and to distinguish causes and effects.

To conclude I would like to make a few remarks about human relations in the didactic process. I often have the feeling of being looked upon as the *expert*. I am the one they asked for to give them *mayele* ('intelligence'). This is a complicated situation. From a European point of view I tend to stress my own restrictions. I try to make them feel that I am one of them, searching together with them, but in their view they need leaders. They do not ask this leader to impose, but to show the way as clearly as possible. They expect you to know what you are talking about instead of being someone wandering with them in the darkness. So they are always a bit distant, although it is difficult to determine whether this is because you are supposed to be a leader or because of the colour of your skin.

Anyway, one of the implications is that people will hardly ever disagree with you, but as soon as you have turned your back they do what they think is best. For example, a group from the course had to look for a field. Someone suggested a plot, and although I did not find it such a good place I agreed in order not to discourage or offend him. But this meant that all the others also immediately agreed. I was satisfied. Everything was settled and I was glad everyone agreed so wholeheartedly. To my amazement I found the next week that they had started working on a field somewhere else. I found out that they all had that place in mind the other day but they did not dare to say it, not wanting to offend me!

A last notion concerns remarks you should or should not make. You should always make remarks in general terms, and if you have to make personal, critical remarks, do so only in private. Take the man aside, then you can say everything to him you want and he will accept it. But pointing out his weakness in public is really *'soni mingi'* ('a shame'). The people do not like conflict situations. They will always try to avoid problems. They will try to arrange things through a third person rather than speak openly. When you make a critical remark in public you cut off the path for further dialogue.

A POSTSCRIPT

I notice, looking through what I have written, the general impression I give is rather negative. It is of course difficult to say positive things when you are asked to write about your problems. Yet in spite of all these problems, or perhaps even thanks to them, I really feel at home in Basankusu and I regard my being here and my work as meaningful. So much so that I decided to renew my contract for another three years.

11 A DUTCH WOMAN AMONGST KIRDI WOMEN

Nicolien Wassenaar

KIRDI LIFE

I have been working for one-and-a-half years as a *co-ordinatrice de l'animation féminine/familiale au Centre de Coordination et d'Appui des Centres de Formation de Jeunes Agriculteurs.* That's quite a mouthful, but it simply means that I am trying to set up a programme for women in Young Farmer Training Centres in the northern part of Cameroon.

This part of Cameroon has a Sahelian climate, with a short rainy season during June, July and August that gives about 700 mm of rainfall, and a long dry season, which makes agriculture complicated, to say the least. The Northern Province has a mixed population. There are Muslims, who own the best pieces of land and occupy nearly all the administrative jobs; they exercise great influence. Then there are the Kirdi, which come from different tribes. The Kirdi are in general poor, and they live in difficult circumstances. They have no power whatsoever. Everything to be done for them needs the permission of the Muslims, which means that it is the Muslims who decide what or what does not happen to the Kirdi. Education of the Kirdi often includes an attempt to make them aware of the circumstances in which they live. Obviously this type of education can be risky for the dominative position of the Muslims.

The percentage of illiteracy in the north is still pretty high. There are not many schools and there is a lack of transportation. Moreover, parents need the children to help in the fields or to herd goats and sheep.

The biggest problem here in the north is the shortage of water. In the dry season, women have to cover long distances to get any water. Often there is a complete lack of water, or if there is water, it will be full of disease germs. Most of the common diseases, like polio, hepatitis, diphteria, helminthiases, dysentry and bilharziasis are caused by contaminated water. Health centres are quite rare in most areas and even if there are any, they do not have the necessary medicines. The staff is usually not sufficiently trained. Housing conditions are still poor and simple. Agriculture is only possible for a short time each year and yields are totally dependant on the amount of rainfall. At the beginning of the rainy season there often is a lack of food. Sometimes the millet stocks are insufficient or even finished. The same applies to groundnuts, one of the rare sources of proteins here in the north. Vegetables are usually completely finished, and fruit of any kind is rare in most areas. All in all, one is confronted here

120

with poor nutrition, unhygienic conditions and nearly all diseases imaginable. Clearly the people's health, especially that of the small children, is very poor. Consequently the death rate is terribly high. A child suffering from malnutrition that catches measles does not have much chance of surviving.

YOUNG FARMER TRAINING CENTRES

The Young Farmer Training Centres are situated in these rural areas. The main co-ordinating and supporting office is based in Maroua, one of the bigger cities in the province. This centre exists since 1977. The staff consists of a Cameroonian director with a degree in agriculture, a Frenchman, who is an educational adviser, his Cameroonian counterpart, and me. I am responsible for the women's work. Formerly the centres operated without any supervision or support, but when the number of centres increased, the need for a co-ordinator grew. Apart from providing co-ordination and support for the training centres, the co-ordinating centre makes field studies to assess the need for new centres. It also evaluates programmes executed by the established farmer training centres, and maintains contact with other agricultural organizations.

The six training centres, the first of which was established in 1969, are spread over the whole northern region of the province, which means a lot of travelling for the co-ordinator. I have to cover distances varying from 18 to 320 km to reach the centres. Each Young Farmer Training Centre recruits married couples from the local area as trainees, which means that they are able to stay in their home region. Every year, twenty-five couples are recruited. The trainees must be originally from the area, they should be married and they should be between twenty and thirty years old. Furthermore, they should be farmers, possess a piece of land and have a good reputation in their home village. It is not necessary that they be literate.

Two or three couples are chosen from each village in an area, in close co-operation with the traditional village chiefs and heads of clans. They stay at the centre for one agricultural season, which is about ten months. There they have a modest house at their disposal and they are allowed to take with them children under ten. Every couple gets a piece of land, where the husband and wife work together. The main crops of the area, cotton, millet, sorghum and groundnuts, are cultivated by the trainees under the supervision and with the help of the staff. Here animal traction is used to till the land. Most of the training takes place directly in the fields, although some theory is taught as well.

The main aim of the centres is 'to improve the agricultural methods and production by means of practical and theoretical teaching in order to obtain a higher standard of living'. Higher production means a higher income, thus creating the possibility of buying meat, oil, fish and clothes and of constructing a better house and sending children to school. In addition to the agricultural programme, women get special education in hygiene, health, child care, nutrition and sewing. Attention is also paid to rural economy, home economics and civics.

Training is executed by the staff of the centre. The director is responsible for the management of the centre; the 'chef de ferme' for the agricultural part, and the 'chef de suivi' follows the former trainees for two years after they have returned to their villages. Normally each centre also has an *animatrice* (organizer). She is responsable for the women's work in the centres.

The agricultural part of the training has been running since 1969, but not much attention was paid to the wives of the trainees. To remedy this deficiency the co-ordinating centre asked for a Dutch volunteer, to establish the women's work in the centres in close collaboration with the Cameroonian staff. So I arrived in Maroua in September 1979. I had two years of experience with a women's programme in West Cameroon, which was extremely different from the North. My job description required that I 'co-ordinate the women's work in the centres' and 'supervise the animatrices working there'.

A PROGRAMME ON PAPER

When I arrived in Maroua I found the situation to be quite different from what was known at the offices in The Hague and Yaounde. First of all, the programme for the women's work was stated in rather broad terms and only one centre had an animatrice. That was it: no material, no fixed outline for the programme, nothing.

After a quick introductory visit to each centre, I decided it was necessary to draw up a preliminary plan for the coming year. This plan had to include a working programme and a task-description for the centres. To me, the most important thing to begin with was to carry out a field study of each centre to discover the main problems in each area. I needed some ideas about the possibilities and, last but not least, I had to know what the women themselves wanted to learn. Furthermore, it was necessary for me to build up regular contacts with the centres' staff and to find out what they had in mind. Together we would draw up a preliminary programme to be tried out during short courses at some of the centres. At the same time, it seemed necessary to do research for the development of didactic and pedagogical means and materials adapted to the North. I also had to find animatrices who were willing to work in rural areas. Contacts with organizations and services around the centres dealing with aspects of women's work or health had to be built up. Evaluation during and at the end of the programme was needed to adapt the programme and to ensure a better continuation. This whole process was complicated by problems of transport and because of the different circumstances of each centre.

STROLLING AROUND

I arrived just after the rainy season. The roads were bad put passable. I wanted to visit the centres regularly to make contact with the staff and especially the director. That way I hoped to get an idea of the way the various centres were run. I spent up to a week at each centre, living in a small *boukarou* (traditional dwelling) and eating with the director and his family. I tried to discuss as much as possible with the staff. I paid informal visits on the trainees and the wife of the director. When I came across objects or actions I had never seen before, I asked for explanations, which they were always willing to give. In this way I got a lot of information about the conditions of daily life. During the evenings informal discussions about all sorts of subjects and especially about life in Holland helped to built up some good contacts. I tried to find out what they considered to be the important subjects in the programme and how it should be organized at their centre. As soon as they found out that it was not me who decided what should be in the programme, it appeared that they had a lot of ideas and thoughts about it and they were quite willing to discuss them.

Unfortunately it was not possible, due to the large distances, to build up good contacts with all the centres. The effect of this showed itself clearly later on.

At three centres, Goyang, Moulvouday and Guetale, where I came often and regularly, I was able to build up good relations with the staff. Activities were easy to organize, discussions were open and the staff felt free to explain their meaning or to come with their own ideas. They felt involved and responsible for the programme. I was not able, however, to visit the other centres, Dana and Dadjamka, regularly, and as a consequence the staff were rather distant toward me. They left all initiatives and arrangements to me. They did not know what to expect from me.

It was also important to maintain these contacts regularly, so the second year I spent more time at Dana and Dadjamka, but then the first three centres complained that I had turned my back on them.

HEALTH CENTRES AND MISSIONS

Our training centres are no isolated spots on the map. They function in the locally prevailing socio-economic environment, with trainees coming from and returning to that very environment. In these areas there have been organizations, services and authorities in existence for many years. I am a volunteer and I will not always stay here. The existing services, however, deal continually with problems of daily life. It seemed quite worthwhile to me to get in touch with these institutions and possibly to involve them in the training programme.

During my first visits to the different institutions I was nearly always accompanied by a staff member of the training centre. The services seemed quite interested to participate in the programme. The main reason for the interest was, in my opinion, that they could reach at one spot a fixed group of twenty-five women; normally they would not have been able to do so. These women in their turn would transfer the information to their villages. There was really two sides to it: to introduce the organization or service to the women, and to introduce the women to the service, from which they could benefit later on, back in their villages.

When we decided to give a short course at the centre in Moulvoudaye, we included the subject prenatal care in the programme. Together with the director, we went to the nearby health centre to ask if the midwife would help us with this topic since she was specially trained in that subject and knew the region, the language and the traditional customs. She was very willing to assist and saw it also as a chance to introduce herself and the health centre to the women, because these women were not at all used to visiting a health centre.

THE SULTAN OF MAKARY

Apart from relations in and around the centres, there were also contacts with higher administrative levels of local government. I was introduced to them by the Cameroonian director of the co-ordinating centre, who knew them quite well and who had many 'friends' among them. Therefore, whenever it was necessary for me to contact these heads of services or other official persons, I always asked him to be my intermediary.

When I began the field study for the centre under construction at Ngouma, it was the director who introduced me to the traditional leader of the area, the Sultan of Makary. He knew him quite well, and he explained the programme and asked permission for me to talk with the women of that region. This also had to do with the Muslim attitude about the man-woman relationship. It is very uncommon that a woman talks directly with a high-ranking man. After this good introduction, the sultan invited me to start working with his own wives, and the later visits passed without any problems and with his full co-operation.

'TALKING WITH WOMEN? WHO ON EARTH DOES THAT'

The northern part of Cameroon is a bit special concerning relations between men and women. In general, because of the Muslim influence, it is a man's country. Well-educated women are rare. If children are sent to school at all, the boys are given preference, seldom the girls. They always stay at home, helping to take care of the other brothers and sisters, or working in the fields. In the cities, this attitude is changing gradually. In rural areas it still is very difficult, and sometimes impossible, to find a woman who can speak some French. As a consequence, most jobs are filled by men.

This makes things difficult for me as a woman who is dealing with women's work but is always obliged to discuss and arrange the women's programme with men. Sometimes the men do not even understand that I really want to talk to the women to get information from them directly, because here it is the man who knows everything and who takes decisions.

One day the agriculturist and I went to Hina, where a new centre is to be constructed, to arrange a meeting with the men and women. The purpose of this visit was to get information about how they practise agriculture and the conditions of daily life in Hina. We fixed a date. They promised to call the men and women together. When we arrived, all the men were there, well-dressed and ready to talk, but not one woman was present. When I asked for the women, the men were very astonished that I really thought it worthwhile talking to women, because nobody ever talks with women about 'important' subjects like a study for a programme. We started discussions with the men and finally, in the afternoon, the organizers of the meeting managed to get about ten women together with an interpreter. This was a man, because none of the women spoke any French.

The chief of the village wanted to participate in the discussion, too, making the situation only more complicated: women are not allowed to face the chief, so they sat with their backs towards him. Because I was a white woman, I was asked to sit next to the chief and to start talking. It is difficult enough to talk through an interpreter but you can perhaps imagine how much worse it is if you cannot see the reaction on the faces of your audience. So I asked permission to put my seat in the other direction, facing the women. Then the discussion really began. I was interested in the routine of their daily life, which was already a bit strange idea for them since it is so 'normal'. I had to explain that I really needed this information since I was not from their village and region. I told them that life was quite different in the place where I was born and that I had to know their circumstances of life to be able to make a good programme for them. They understood and were quite willing to tell me everything I wanted to know.

Then another problem arose. The interpreter translated my questions correctly, but then he started to give the answers himself. 'Why ask the women something if the answer is clear and he knew it also?'. So again I had to explain that I understood he was capable of replying, but that I really wanted to have the information from the women themselves. He accepted my argument but was still surprised and felt strange about it.
There are more examples of such difficulties. In general, life and work at the centres is structured in such a way that it is pretty much the same as life in the village.
When I arrived I started discussions with the wives of the trainees in the centres. These talks provided information about their daily life, needs and problems. It was clear that they were not at all happy with their situation. After some time I discovered why. In their villages they work for a large part on their husband's field, assisting him in farming. This is done mainly in the mornings or when there is a lot of work. Apart from that, they have their private field, where they cultivate some small food crops. Part of these crops is used for the family and part is sold to make some money. With the millet, they brew millet beer, which is sold as well. With the money they make they are able to buy some basic needs like clothes, cooking oil, salt and fish or meat.
In the centres they are obliged to work together with their husband all day

long on one field, where they only cultivate cotton, millet and groundnuts. This led to the strange situation that they did not have any money to buy the necessary things for the housekeeping. Nor were they able to prepare a good meal, since they could not grow vegetables or beans, and they could not sell anything to buy fish or meat.

When I discussed it with the centres' staffs and those of the co-ordinating centre, they were very surprised to hear about this. They gave a reasonable explanation: 'Nobody ever talked with the women to find out what they wanted. Since we are men, we couldn't do it, because a man doesn't talk about these kind of things with women, and we never had a woman who could talk to them.' After hearing the problem, however, they were quite willing to change things because they saw the need. They had just been ignorant of the fact and had never bothered to ask whether the women agreed with the 'normal' state of affairs.

MAKING A START

Moulvoudaye, Dana, Dadjamka, Goyang, Guetale and Ngouma are the small villages where the training centres are located. The distances between Maroua and these villages vary from 18 to 320 km, which means that I have to travel very much. Because of these large distances I could not manage to visit all centres regularly. Yet this is necessary to built up good contacts. Each centre is situated in quite a different area with a different tribe. Consequently, you have to visit every village to get a good idea of the conditions of daily life. Most of the time it was not possible to work intensively in one place. The only solution, which I can sometimes arrange, is to stay a whole week in a centre and organize an intensive, practical programme for that week.

Another problem was that the centres had been functioning already for some years without a women's programme and this new aspect had to be fitted in somewhere. But agriculture was much more important for the centres and there was no money in the budget for the women's programme. Fortunately the director of the co-ordinating centre, as well as most of the directors of the other centres, were interested to discuss this difficulty and to try to find a solution. We decided to start slowly and to built up the programme step by step, by trying out various activities. The staff participated fully in the organization of these activities. When they saw that both men and women showed interest, they became enthusiastic and they were willing to put in even more effort.

ANIMATRICE IN JEANS

One of the major problems was, and still is, to find good animatrices to run the programme in the centres. We do not demand many qualifications: they should speak and write some French, come originally from the area and be able to speak the local language. Furthermore they have to be interested in the work and willing to stay at the centres, in the 'brousse' (bush). It was rather difficult to find a woman or a girl who could speak and write some French. Girls with some schooling often leave the villages to find a job in the city.

At a certain moment we got a nice 'present' from Yaounde. They sent us an animatrice for the centre in Moulvoudaye. She got the job through her contacts with a highly placed person, but she was not at all suitable for this type of work. She was seventeen years old, educated in a big city, not interested in the job, not willing to work at all – certainly not in the brousse – and could not speak the local language. Nevertheless the whole staff tried to give her some education and supported her.

In the mornings she nearly always slept in the office since she did the 'real animation' in the evenings. I took her one week with me to Moulvoudaye, which is a bit isolated, to work with the women. Everyday she showed up in an evening dress or in jeans, which caused much surprise among the women and the centre's staff, not to mention me. She did not prepare any lesson.

Back in Maroua, she told everybody once more that she did not want to stay in that 'brousse-place' and started to come late to the office or even not to come at all. Because of her contact, we were in a difficult position to undertake some action. Eventually the house in the centre meant for the animatrice was repaired so that there was then no reason for her not to go there. That was it: she refused to go. She was dismissed and we were rid of her.

DO NA WE, NAK BOURA WASSOU, MBALAÏ, ALLA CLAVIA, ASKISSOU, NDJAMNA

Six centres. Six different areas with different customs, habits and traditions, and six different languages. Complication in multiples of six.

The official language in the north is French, which is spoken in the cities and sometimes by one or two men in the villages. The common language is Foulfouldé, spoken by all the Foulbe and nearly all the men and some women of the other tribes. There are many tribes, each one with its own language, which is often the only language the women of that tribe can speak. Together in all the centres there are probably about five of the 150 women who can speak some Foulfouldé; none of them speaks French. The consequence is that I have always depended on an interpreter, a different one in each centre. Most of the time a man, since it is difficult to find a woman who can translate. Because of the six different languages it was impossible for me to learn all of them.

The disadvantage of working through an interpreter, even a good one, is that it is never possible for you to have direct contact with the person you are talking to. You always have to wait until your question is translated, watch the faces, wait till the answer or answers are translated again, react, and so on. I find it very difficult to react directly to something that is said, and I often miss part of the answers or reactions. Much depends on the interpreter: if you find a good one you can manage.

128

DAILY LIFE: PROBLEMS, NEEDS AND WISHES

Not only do the languages differ from centre to centre but also the customs, traditions and the way of life. The housing and food, for instance, also vary from place to place. To be able to design a programme that is relevant to daily life, it is necessary for me to know and to learn as much as possible about the women's circumstances and way of life. Therefore I made a questionnaire, with many questions about childcare, nutrition, women's agriculture, water, diseases and the like. Armed with this list, I went to the centres, where meetings and discussions were organized with former trainees in the villages and with the trainees in the centres. I always started to explain why I was there and that it was necessary for me to know their way of life, circumstances, problems, needs and wishes to be able to draw up a programme that reflects their needs. I also explained that in my country life was quite different, so that although some of my questions might appear a bit silly to them, I really did have to ask them.

My questionnaire started with a question about the first thing they did when they got up. When they answered, for instance, 'to get water', I could ask where they got it from, if they had to go far to get it, and if the quality was good. When they said 'to prepare the morning meal', I could continue by asking what they were eating and how they prepared this food, and where they got the ingredients from. If they mentioned bathing the children, I could ask how they did that, if the child was well and how often it was ill. In this way we slowly went through the whole daily routine of life. This provided me with a lot of information.

Afterwards I would ask them to show me their house and compound, if they liked. In general they were very proud to do so. They were pleased with the attention given to them and quite willing to give all the information they could. During these meetings they would tell of their major problems and needs; they knew very well what they wanted and what in fact was attainable for them.

> When I was talking about clean water with the women of the Dadjamka area, where they really have a water problem, some of them asked about methods of getting good drinking-water. Even before I could answer, another woman replied that I should not talk about filters and that kind of thing because they were too expensive for them and not available in the villages.

After I had gathered all this information from the women, I discussed the results with the centre's director to get their views on the programme. Then I went to missions, health centres and hospitals to ask about their problems and to get information about the diseases of the area. I also studied the teaching materials they used. The meaning of all these activities was to adapt the programme in each of the centres as much as possible to the existing programmes, and to use the same kind of materials. This information was quite useful and also prevented some mistakes.

> At the mission in Koza I had some discussions about the programme and about visual aids. The sister in charge of the women's work showed me a booklet that had been developed there over five years and that was ex-

tremely well adapted to the area. I was enthusiastic and I asked her for the address where I could get it. (I managed to get it for the nearby centre.) She also told me a lot about special problems existing in the area.

Everywhere I came I heard about vaccination programmes for the children, to protect them against particular diseases. So I thought it might be a good idea to have this as topic in the programme. However I found out from the health centre near Dadjamka that it was impossible for them to vaccinate there: they did not have the means to keep the vaccins cool enough during transport.

Without the collaboration of the women and all the services it would never have been possible for me to gather all this information in such a short time.

Back in Maroua, full of impressions and information, I sorted out all data to get an overview of the situation. I then drew up an outline of the programme, divided into the subjects hygiene in the village; nutrition; health of mother and child; diseases; and sewing. This outline was discussed again with the directors of the centres. When necessary it was changed, and only then was it introduced at the centres. By working in this way, having several contacts with which to discuss the programme, I tried to avoid certain very real risks. As I come from another culture, with other ideas, norms and values, and being the only woman in the whole organization of the centres, there was always the risk of working too much of my own background and point of view into the programme. I did not want that, but I was all too aware that some traces would inevitably creep in. Therefore exchange of ideas with other services and critics, self-criticism, and regular testing and evaluation of the programme were quite indispensible.

BE CAREFUL WITH THEORY

The programme was more or less on paper, but I still had to answer the question of how to present it in such a way that the women would understand it, become interested in it and benefit from it as much as possible. I had to keep in mind that none of them could read or write. Very few of them had ever been to school and they were not at all used to teaching situations. Their world is small and limited to the village they lived in. At best they are familiar with the village they come from or with the village their parents came from. The most important things for them are to cultivate enough food to stay alive and to have enough to eat for the whole year. This work has to be done under harsh conditions and they are always struggling to keep themselves and their children alive, to get their house repaired, to get water and firewood and to earn a small amount of money to buy the basic needs for their housekeeping. The programme had to correspond to these needs and offer improvements where possible, according to their wishes.

Since agriculture is one of the most important pursuits in the areas, I could not plan many activities during the agricultural season. Then the women were nearly the whole day in the field, so I had to plan most of the activities during the

130

hot, dry season. This was not the only case of seasons affecting the planning.

In the part of the programme concerned with health I included a lesson about malaria. It turned out that this part was to be given sometime in December, when the worst period for malaria is just over. Malaria reaches its climax during the rainy season, in July, August and September. I realized that this lesson, in which prevention and treatment of malaria were handled, should be planned before this season to match the topic and the actual situation.

The same applies to the other subjects. To talk about birthing and later about pregnancy is not logical; nor does it make sense to explain how to prepare a dish with fresh vegetables when they are not available at that time. To be able to make the programme logical and relevant, knowledge of the peoples' circumstances is indispensable.

FLIP-CHART, DISCUSSION OR DEMONSTRATION

I still had to find out which didactical methods or means were best suited to the women and the situation. Together with the directors of the Goyang, Guetale and Moulvoudaye centres we set up an intensive programme of one week for each centre, to test various ways of teaching. This programme included lessons of different levels and methods, for example a demonstration, a theoretical lesson, and use of a flip-chart, participation of the women, participation of men and women, and practical lessons.

We also invited others to participate, for example a midwife, a sister from the mission and a health agent. We discussed the contents and objectives of the lesson with everybody and the trainees were informed about the coming activities. These weeks really were strenuous but I learned a lot from it and the results were useful in drawing up the programme and in gathering materials for the women's work.

FILTERING WATER AND WITCHCRAFT

If a topic is not directly related to the situation of the trainees, interest disappears after about fifteen minutes. Questions are then never asked. If it does not concern them, they do not get involved in the subject.

Someone was giving a lesson about the importance of clean water, which concerned the trainees very much. Then she started talking about getting water from the well instead of the river and about filtering water with sophisticated filters. Since these filters were not available in the surrounding area and, if bought in the city, were too expensive for the trainees, they lost interest. The women began attending to the children and did not pay any attention to what was said.

In contrast the director of the centre decided to talk about the witchcraft of some so-called doctors, since it is very common for people to spend money uselessly on these practices. He knew the situation and the so-called doctors, and he was able to give some examples of trainees and other well known persons who went to them for a consultation, paid a lot of money and did not get any relief. He gave an example and asked the trainees what happened. Since it was directly related to their situation they got involved in the subject and participated fully in what became a sprightly discussion.

BALANCING MEALS AND BATHING BABIES

The women have a very practical outlook on life, so long, theoretical lessons do not have much effect. Halfway through a lesson trainees often get tired, as they are not used to sitting down for such a long time. Because they have difficulty in remembering what is said we decided to give only short theoretical introductions and thereafter to be as practical as possible.

A lesson about the balanced meal started with a short introduction and explanation of the three food groups by using a flannel board. With the flannel figures they composed a balanced meal, which was demonstrated and prepared directly afterwards in one of their kitchens. During this demonstration nearly all responsibility was given to the women. Each one had to bring a small quantity of millet and vegetables and they had to prepare it under supervision of the animatrice. After some difficulties we noticed that the easiest way was just to say what needed to be done, leaving the responsibility to the women to organize things for themselves and to divide the work. (A high-placed person in the group cannot be told to grind the millet, that is a task for the one who has a lower social standing). In this way they felt more responsible for 'their meal' and could be proud of it afterwards.

With demonstrations some caution appeared to be necessary.

When the animatrice gave a demonstration of the baby-bath, she borrowed a bowl and some soap from the director's wife. Afterwards the women commented that for them it was impossible to bath their baby in the manner shown because they did not have a similar bowl and that kind of soap. Obviously we had to use things that they have readily at hand, such as a big calebash. If we are forced to use borrowed materials we suggest and ask them at the same time what other materials could also be used.

I remember making another mistake in a sewing lesson.

We were going to make a baby's dress. I thought I had chosen an easy pattern, but after a while I noticed that, because of the number of pieces, it was a bit complicated. Nevertheless it did not give too many problems, and the animatrice and me were easily able to avoid mistakes. The results were not bad at all, but I realized that because of the difficulties caused by the number of pieces, they would never manage to reproduce the 'simple dress' alone at home. The pattern was simply too complicated for them. The next time we chose a simpler dress, which did not require so much work and was easy to reproduce afterwards without the use of a pattern.

A NIVAQUINE TABLET WITHOUT A GROOVE

Some subjects cannot be treated in a practical way without using visual aids: trainees recognize situations earlier when they see them; they also remember it better later on. Probably this has to do with the very real and practical aspects of their existence. To imagine and to think abstractly without seeing the objects is difficult for them. Two points must be kept in mind, however. The animatrice has to know exactly how to use the visual aids and the material has to be adapted to the situation.

A flip-chart about the weaning of children and child-feeding showed a mother sitting on a table using a plate and spoon. Some foodstuff, which was unknow in the region, was also shown. As the women possess neither tables, nor plates and spoons, the pictures did not tell them much. Since there were no better images available we developed some ourselves showing a mother in the clothes of the region, sitting on a piece of wood and using a small calebash-spoon and calebash to feed the child with foodstuffs of the area. This worked quite effectively.

It was necessary for me to develop some educational materials myself, but I soon made mistakes.

I made a small poster consisting of only pictures about the use of nivaquine to prevent malaria. The nivaquine tablets were shown on the poster as small white circles. When I explained it to the women, they remarked that these were not nivaquine tablets because they did not have the groove in the middle so that they could be broken in two! A very small point, but not insignificant.

It took about one-and-a-half years to get the programme established. Materials were developed, tested and improved. By trial and error I learned what to do and how to do it. What has given me the most satisfaction, however, is the flow of free comments, remarks and criticisms from the women, which shows that they do not just blindly accept what the 'white man' considers good for them.

12 ON THE BATTLEFIELD OF WISHES AND NEEDS

Goof Bus

PROJECTS IN PROFILE

My impressions are based on my experiences with two different projects: the Agricultural Settlement Project in the Bangem-Bakossi area of Cameroon, and the Village-cattle Improvement Scheme in Ivory Coast.

The Agricultural Settlement Project in Cameroon is a 'co-financed' project of the Dutch Ministry of Technical Co-operation and CEBEMO[1]. The local Diocese of Buea acted as the executive body. The project started in 1972. I was project manager from 1974–1976.

The project consisted of a Farmers Training Centre, a Home Economics Centre and a Settlement Programme. At the training centre young Bakossi men were trained in basic agricultural techniques in a one-year course. After this training they would obtain a plot on land ceded to the settlement scheme by the local chiefs. During the entire project period of eight years only twenty young farmers were trained and were allowed to settle on a plot of land. Each farmer got 10 hectares. In the Home Economics Centre young girls from the Bakossi region followed a one-year course in needlework, dressmaking, handicrafts, cooking, babycare, and so on. The centre has given a total of four courses.

The settlers-to-be were between 20 and 25 years of age. There are 8 clans living in this region, and to avoid rivalry among those clans, each clan was represented in the newly recruited group settlers. Application forms were sent to all village chiefs. After a first selection about half of the candidates are turned away. The other half do a simple written test. Of those doing the test, 20 settlers are chosen. The number of vacancies is limited because there are only 20 farms available.

The cattle improvement scheme in Ivory Coast began in 1972 and is still expanding its activities. This scheme is mainly an advisory service to inform the farmers on how to improve their cattle. The Extension Service consists of 200 Livestock Assistants, who are in daily contact with the farmers. These assistants are supervised by 30 Assistant Livestock Officers, who in turn are supervised by 5 Livestock Officers.

1 CEBEMO is the Centrale voor Bemiddeling bij Medefinanciering van Ontwikkelingsprogramma's; or in English, the Catholic Organization for Joint Financing of Development Programmes in the Netherlands.

134

I worked on the project from 1977 until 1981. As head of the socio-economic section, which was responsible for such activities as socio-economic research, training of the extension workers and advising them in the field.

The age of the trainee *encadreurs* and *chefs de secteur* varied between 23 and 50 years, but most of them were between 20 and 30 years old. Trainees came from all over the country. The basic training course lasts three months.

To train as an encadreur the candidate has to be able to speak French and one of the three local languages, or the lingua franca, Dioula. Primary school has to have been completed; further education is to the candidate's advantage. The selection procedure for candidates is lengthy, consisting of a written application, a test and an interview. The number of candidates finally accepted is related to the need for encadreurs at that moment.

KEEPING THE TRAIN ON THE RAILS

In the Plan of Operations of the Cameroon settlement scheme no provision was made for running costs. It was assumed by the donor, the Dutch Government, that these expenses were to be paid by the diocese or covered by the produce of the production plot of the project. But after two years it became clear that these costs were too heavy a burden on the diocese's budget. Moreover the yield of the production plot fell far short of the initial expectations. Consultations with the Dutch Government about the running expenses brought no solution to the problem, so the diocese was forced to finance the running costs from remaining funds earmarked for capital investments. Another financing problem arose when at the end of the first phase of the project the diocese realized that it had to prefinance all further expenditures before the Dutch Government would remit the final instalment. The amount of these expenditures ran up to more than US $40 000. The result was that several activities in the project had to be suspended.

To safeguard the continuation of the project the diocese tried to persuade the Cameroon Government to take over the project. This attempt failed, however, as the Cameroon Government, under its own policy, did not consider itself responsible for the running of a project begun by a private institution.

The cattle improvement scheme in the Ivory Coast had its financial problems too, but there poor financial administration and not lack of resources was the problem. The scheme is composed of several sub-projects, each of which has its own donor. The Government of the Ivory Coast has to pre-finance all expenditures and is reimbursed by the donors after submitting the pre-paid bills. But often the government administration either forwards the bills only after much delay (1–2 years) or even sends them to the wrong donor. At the end of 1980 the amount still to be reimbursed had accumulated to more than four million US dollars. As a result the Ministry of Animal Husbandry ran into an acute liquidity problem, causing a temporary shut-down of many activities.

The settlement project in Cameroon suffered from severe organizational

difficulties in its starting period, because of the lack of clear descriptions of every one's function and responsibilities. For instance, for several reasons it was very difficult for the local missionary, who had initiated the project, to withdraw and leave the execution of the project to the project manager appointed by the Dutch Government. As this priest had a great influence on the local population, the manager became more and more isolated, resulting in a delay of the training programme for young farmers of at least two years.

THE PRICE OF POLITICS AND IDEOLOGY

One of the reasons why the settlement project in Cameroon more or less failed was the tension, and even conflicts, among the different local clans. The Cameroon government decided to allocate land to settlers graduating from the project. But the area allotted had been the subject of a dispute between two adjacent villages, each belonging to a different clan, for many, many years. By ceding the land to the project this conflict was solved, but unfortunately it created a new problem. The settlers living on that land no longer belonged to a village community, so that they did not fall under a local authority any longer. Consequently, problems among them that would be normally handled by the chiefs according to their own traditional law and customs had to be solved by the project manager, who was, of course, totally incompetent to deal with such matters.

Differences in ideology were the root of a problem I met on the cattle improvement scheme on the Ivory Coast. The local authorities and I differed in our interpretation of the project's aims. The main objective of the project was, and still is, to diminish the import of meat by increasing local production. Considerable emphasis was put on production and hardly none on improving the standard of living of the individual farmers. According to this policy the government concentrates its efforts on those farmers who are in the best position to achieve a high production. These relatively big farmers are provided with all kinds of facilities, such as fenced-off, improved pasture land and subsidized feeds. From the macro-economic point of view this policy may be justified, but in my view foreign aid should primarily benefit the poorest of a community, so this policy was unacceptable to me. Talking about this with government officials was hardly possible and often created irritation. This is because the expatriate is easily seen by the officials as an ethical hypocrite who, having a good salary himself, dares to tell them not to forget their poor. The officials claim to be well aware of the desperate situation of the poor, but give priority to the economic development of the country as a whole, which in the government's opinion can only be achieved by stimulating those who have got the means to increase production.

Expatriate teachers at secondary schools are not allowed to discuss politics with their pupils. When, for instance, during lessons on social geography the students try to discuss the government's development policy, the teacher is expected to discourage this at once. One should only talk in general terms about the government-initiated development schemes, but one should never explain the way in which these schemes are executed and who finally benefits from them.

NEEDS, DEEDS AND EXPECTATIONS

The question of educational needs arises in relation to the training of newly appointed cattle extension workers. They have all completed primary school, but much of this basic knowledge is long forgotten. They are often poor in arithmetic and reading. Spatial understanding is hardly developed and when observing a problem they do not make the connection between cause and effect.

Before being placed at their duty stations the extension workers get a basic training of three months in animal husbandry. They are taught how to construct a kraal, how to vaccinate, how to treat cattle against internal and external parasites and how to register the number of births and deaths each month. This course, mainly aimed at teaching practical skills, is insufficient. For instance, because of a lack of thorough basic general knowledge, the monthly figures on births and deaths are not interpreted, so that an unusual increase or decrease in the number of animals is not noticed, and, consequently, the necessary measures are not taken in time. The data are dutifully collected, indeed, but this serves no purpose at all. The vade-mecum, the extension workers' handbook, is hardly consulted and mostly it disappears in a corner under a layer of dust. This vade-mecum should be consulted regularly so that the extensionists correct their own mistakes, and they do make many mistakes, for instance when they try to find the right age of the cattle. They often vaccinate in the wrong way, too, and they do not always use the prescribed dose of insecticide against ticks.

In-service training courses are not always suitable to correct these mistakes as the extensionists do not like courses in which they are taught about things they already presume to know. They prefer to learn something new. Nevertheless, during a recent in-service training course it was possible to arouse some interest in subjects dealt with in former courses by the method *formation punctuelle*. This means that the instruction starts from a final result, e.g. the change in fertility of a herd of cattle. Once this is identified, the group discusses the factors that may have influenced the fertility either in a positive or a negative way. By this method of teaching several aspects of animal husbandry were dealt with in a more coherent and logical way.

In-service training courses on how to advise farmers have been taught for some years. The extensionists are very keen to attend these classes as they think that these lessons in extension methods will teach them some sociological tricks by which the farmers can be manipulated in a sly way.

The organisers of the initial training course for the extension workers are confronted with the question of what type of course is more important, one based on general knowledge that emphasizes independent and critical thinking or one emphasizing acquisition of technical skills. To answer this question one should know which type of extensionist is more capable of performing his task:

the person who is able to think critically and analytically or the person who can only carry out basic technical procedures without a sense of self-evaluation. To date no clear answer to this question has been found but I am inclined to think that a basic course on general agricultural knowledge followed by thorough supervision in the field and regular in-service training courses is a good answer.

Needs are strongly connected with expectations. What does a student expect of this training? Arousing false expectations may have fatal consequences for a project. This became evident in the settlement project in Cameroon. It was pointed out to the population that the young farmers would get a training in modern agricultural methods, which meant that later on they would work with tractors and all kinds of modern agricultural implements. Moreover, an excellently built school surrounded by experimental fields aroused the expectation that the standard of teaching would be very high and that it would be possible to master all the agricultural problems by means of the knowledge acquired there.

In practice, however, this proved to be different: the use of tractors was reduced to a minimum, so that the young settlers had to do most tillage by hand. This was a very great disappointment for them, especially because growing food crops, and consequently working with a hoe, is considered women's work. Those who had not been so lucky as to be selected as settlers made fun of those who had been. No wonder that after two years more than half the original settlers had disappeared from the project.

The expectations of the domestic science students also differed from those of their teachers. The latter thought to educate young women to play a leading part in their own village community. The girls, however, considered the school as an excellent means to flee the village community and begin as seamstresses in a larger settlement. The girls wanted to learn as much as possible within a very short period. This attitude caused conflicts with the staff. When, for instance, the teachers refused to introduce 'free-hand cutting' and insisted on working to patterns, the students went on strike.

The older people of the village community also had high expectations of the project. After all, their sons would become modern farmers, who would procure them a comfortable old age. They presumed that the project had accepted total responsibility for the education and settlement of their children. This attitude went so far that they even refused to contribute to the bride-price of their sons, one of their traditional responsibilities.

THE DIPLOMA DISEASE

It is common knowledge that in developing countries much value is attached to certificates. This is quite understandable, because holding a certificate is the only way someone can reach positions that provide a higher standard of living. The teachers take advantage of this situation, for the students have a strong motivation to work hard and they are eager to learn. There are no difficulties in preserving order at school, which, of course, also has to do with the traditional respect for parents.

Attaching too much value to certificates has its drawbacks, however: it strongly promotes corruption. Many boys at secondary schools get high marks by paying hush-money; girls try to do so by making love to their teachers. Moreover, they concentrate on gathering knowledge, on simply learning facts. Therefore many subjects are learnt by heart and the students easily forget that it is also necessary to try to understand what they learn. This approach is understandable, as testing is done in such a way that a certificate is obtained in the first place by knowing much, not by understanding much.

Many Europeans speak slightingly of the value Africans attach to certificates. However it is my opinion that for the African this is a justifiable idea and I think that every course must be rounded off with an official certificate. This is not to say that the curricula should not be improved. I simply want to stress that our Western European ideas about achievement and diploma's are not always applicable to the situation in developing countries.

COUNTERPART OR PARTNER?

To close, I want to touch on the relation between counterpart and expatriate. This is often a delicate, problematic one. There may be many causes for this. For instance, a local officer of much experience does not like to be seen as a 'pupil' of a young, and often inexperienced, European. Besides, the nature of their mutual authority is not always clear. Problems may also arise when the counterpart is formally responsible to the expatriate but the senior officer of the department that supplies the counterpart continues to exert a strong influence on him. This is even reinforced if that department also pays the counterpart's salary.

Another problem may arise if the counterpart has had another professional training than the expatriate. I, an agricultural sociologist, was assigned an economist. This was partly because there is no agricultural sociologist employed in the Ivory Coast and partly because people with a technical training consider sociology and economics to be much alike.

My counterpart took a great interest in sociological problems, as there are quite some tensions among the several ethnic groups with which we worked. However, this interest did not result from his scientific background, but rather it was a consequence of personal problems in his relations with other groups of the population, for he was a Fullani and there are great racial tensions between the Fullani and the autochthon farmers. The counterpart was strongly inclined toward stereotype thinking, which unfavourably affected the objectivity of a sociological study that he worked on.

To me it is quite important that expatriates and local counterparts see each other as partners working towards development, rather than as rivals who have to take care of each other. There is much to learn from each other. Feelings of superiority or inferiority do not stimulate this process of mutual help and understanding.

140

13 THE ART OF BEGINNING: SOME CONCLUSIONS AND SUGGESTIONS

Wout van den Bor

CAPTIVES IN THE CAVE: INTRODUCTION

Try to imagine the following situation. There is an underground cave with only one entrance to let in the light. There are people in the cave, people who have been chained there since they were born, and who cannot move or even turn their heads. From a great distance behind these captives, a fire sheds light from above into the cave. And between that fire and the captives, high above their heads, there is a path. A brick wall conceals the path from the eyes of the captives. All kinds of people walk along the path behind the wall and they carry bundles that the captives see above the wall. Some people talk on their way, others pass silently.

What can these chained captives see and hear? They can see nothing more than the shadows of themselves and objects, cast upon the wall opposite them by the light of the fire. Let's assume that the prisoners are able to talk to each other. What would they say? It would be quite natural to assume that they believe that their explanations of what they see are correct. Imagine that they can hear echoes of the voices of the passers-by, which bounce off the wall of the cave. Would they not think that the shadows are speaking?

Imagine now that for the first time in his life one of the captives is freed from his chains. He can stand up, walk and turn to look at the light behind him. But the light would surely hurt his eyes, and because of its flare he would not be able to see the objects that until now had been casting shadows on the wall. What do you think he would say if you were to try and explain that until now he had only been seeing things of no importance and that now he is closer to reality and seeing things as they are? If you were to force him to look at the light, his eyes would probably be blinded, and there is a good chance that he would turn away to look at things he has always been able to see. Wouldn't he be absolutely convinced that these are more real than what he saw once freed?

Plato used this parable in his famous work 'Politeia' to illustrate the nature of human life and the limits of human knowledge. Of course, it is impossible to go into the details of Plato's philosophy here, but I believe that this parable is relevant to the subject of this book. You don't need much imagination to realize that the development worker, during the first phase of his work, experiences much the same as Plato's captive, when, for the first time in his life, he is confronted with the blinding light of the fire. The stories in this book are the

141

proof. Ideas and ideals that have long governed the way of thinking are useless or of limited value in the new situation in a developing country. One's knowledge and skills prove to be insufficient or inapplicable. The confrontation with the reality of a developing country is problematic. In the preceding essays the various kinds of problems that may be encountered have been examined in depth. It's a colourful mosaic, a patchwork of problems, experiences and solutions. This jumble of 'sounds' must in some way be arranged into a harmonious composition. I will try to give an outline in this chapter that I hope will show that similarities exist in the different essays. However I do not want to use a very abstract outline, as the reality of development work is indeed very varied and cannot be encased in a theoretical straight-jacket.

In the introduction to this book I mentioned different kinds of beginning problems: problems that have to do with culture and social life, economic problems, problems related to political points of view and philosophies of life, educational stumbling blocks and problems related to the organizational aspects of the project.

The way in which the expatriate development worker handles these problems depends on a number of factors. In the first place, it is important to examine the extent and nature of his knowledge, his technical know-how, for example, and his knowledge of languages, culture and history. Furthermore it is also of great importance to determine whether the expatriate is capable of applying his knowledge or, to be more explicit, whether he possesses not only technical skills but also social skills. Can he repair a machine and supervise a group of people? Last but not least, it is very important to take into consideration the development worker's personality. Does he function well as a person, living and working with others? I realize that this is once again a purely theoretical classification, but it serves the purpose of organizing the expatriate's problems and experiences within a framework. The distinction between 'knowledge', on the one hand, and 'ability and being', on the other hand, will recur frequently in the following discussion, either implicitly or explicitly.

Let's return now to our prisoner who has come face to face with the fact that the situation is very different than that he had anticipated. Once he has become accustomed to the light of new truths, he will notice that the cave from which he came is one of many. The inhabitants of the country where he will be working also live in a 'cave' – a different cave. They too are used to familiar shadows on the wall. Then, one day, the development worker arrives, 'frees them from their chains' and tells them to turn around and look. You can well imagine what will then happen. Confusion and consternation, fear and the urge to return to the old and familiar situation. But that's not as easy as it first seems. The development worker takes them, in a manner of speaking, outside their cave, where they stand, blinking in the bright light. They will have to adapt their way of thinking and acting to the new situation.

I will discuss systematically the problems that the development worker experiences in this situation, with the purpose of helping him prepare himself as well as he can. For his hosts I can do very little. This situation is in my opinion something of a paradox, and rather frustrating. They will have to have faith in

143

this 'foreigner' from the Western world, but especially trust in their own wisdom and experience. I will make no attempt to give a complete picture of the situation in this discussion, that would be beyond my capabilities. I'll just adhere to the basic principle of using examples to discuss a cross-section of the problems that are dealt with in the essays.

STRONGER THAN REASON: THE CULTURAL ISSUE

The Pokot never eat fish. The Turkana clothe themselves in animal skins. Kirdi women must submit to their husband's whims and wishes. People from Western Europe visit the doctor when they are ill. So many different societies, so many different cultures. There are countless ways of defining culture. I have chosen one that in this case serves my purpose: culture is the whole of assumptions, opinions, values and norms that people as members of a certain society have acquired by means of processes of learning and that are pre-conditions for the survival of that society. The Western expatriate encounters a foreign culture and invariably experiences problems.

In their stories all authors indicate that this confrontation occurs. From their experiences we can learn that it is very important – indispensable – to acquire a certain amount of knowledge beforehand about the culture in which you will be working. The problem, however, is that the amount and kind of knowledge you will need differs from culture to culture, country to country and even region to region. Nevertheless, some general guidelines can be distilled from the various experiences. Speaking the local language, for example, is often very important. I am not only referring to a technical command of the language – the dialect – but also to a certain knowledge of the role the language plays in the social life of the people – the sociolect. Furthermore, the importance of religion and it's place in society is often emphasized.

The sense of right and wrong differs between cultures; a certain familiarity with local and common law can forestall many problems. One of the authors has in this respect discussed traditional medicine, food habits, the relationships between men and women, the sense of time, and rules governing hospitality and privacy. Of course it would be virtually impossible to get to know almost everything about these subjects during the relatively short training periods that are common, but some amount of study of such matters would certainly be worthwhile. But is knowing about the culture of the people for and with whom you will be working enough?

The essays have clearly demonstrated that possessing this knowledge is not enough for the beginning development worker. He must be capable of doing something with the knowledge. He must use it, put it into practice. Theoretical mastery of a language is comforting, but you need a certain amount of courage also to speak the language. Knowing that the village chief plays a key role in the village society is gratifying, but you will also have to build up a relationship with the chief and discuss things with him. Knowing that the concept of time in other cultures is completely different to our Western concept of time is an

144

advantage, but you will also have to use this knowledge, for example by having enough patience to wait for the right moment. We have become experts in optimizing time, but have we learned to make time?

Automatically we have now arrived at the subject of your behaviour, the way you act in a new, foreign situation, the subject of 'being'. Each person has his own character, his own personality. It would be an illusion to assume that the minute you set foot in a foreign country, you shed your old skin and are born again as a new person with a different way of looking at the world and behaving towards others. However, a basic approach, a certain mentality that will enable you to meet the new situation with some degree of success, is also important, as is the ability to say nothing and listen. The point is whether you are willing and capable of relativizing and discussing your own ideas and opinions.

Some readers may find my approach to the subject rather tiresome. They will argue: 'What is the good of all this philosophizing. Just say what you mean in practical terms. How should I act, what should I do and what not?' I cannot give them a simple answer because we are dealing with the individual's human feelings and behaviour, which differ in time and place. Many examples of real life situations in which the beginning development worker was faced with distinctive cultural phenomena, before then completely unknown to him, can be found in this book. Theo Groot's experiences with the concept of time and those of Nicolien Wassenaar with the roles of men and women are cases in point; examples of situations in which you have to see the things you were taught as a child to consider 'right' or 'wrong' or 'normal' in a different light.

Perhaps you could best compare an individual's personality with a walled city where all kinds of things are happening. Life in the city, however, is governed by a number of fixed rules and habits. Although the pattern of streets and buildings is gradually changing, the contours remain essentially the same. The inhabitants of the city belong to different groups that are related in specific ways; they understand, complement and need each other. The question now is whether the city council is willing to open the gates in the wall that surrounds the city to outsiders who knock and request that they too be permitted to live in the city. Opening the gates will certainly lead to changes. New people bring new things and ideas. Also some of the inhabitants of the city will want to take a look outside the city and return with new habits, which they will want to adopt in the city. Life in the city will change drastically. You, the beginning development worker, will also be asked time and time again to open the gates of your city, of your old familiar personal world of thoughts and experiences, to visitors who come knocking. Will you open your gates?

Many conclusions can be drawn from the subjects discussed in the various papers, conclusions which no doubt are important for the training of beginning development workers. However, enough treatises on the subject of the profile of the most desirable kind of development worker have already been published. A number of these are listed in the annotated bibliography, which follows this chapter. But I cannot conclude this section without noting that dealing with what is often called 'culture shock' requires, above all, a good knowledge of yourself. This knowledge and the ability to judge and act accordingly are firmly united. This has seldom been expressed as strikingly by anyone as Montaigne in his 'Essays', in which he says, 'We are nearer neighbours to ourselves than the whiteness of snow or the weight of stones are to us: if man does not know himself, how should he know his functions and powers?'

WHITES ARE HONEST: THE SOCIAL ISSUE

Cultural and social life are closely interwoven. When I speak of social problems, discussed by the authors of the various papers, they can hardly be considered independent of the cultural context in which social relationships exist. I have said that it is extremely useful that the beginning development worker acquire some knowledge of the society where he will be working. If he is unable to do this before his departure, time spent familiarizing himself with the society during the first phase of his work on location will certainly be well invested. Time and time again we discover that in projects – very well planned from a technical point of view – absolutely no reference is made to the social context in which the project is to be implemented.

The essays in this book often emphasize the importance of understanding the ways in which people live as a family or household, and of acquiring this knowledge as soon as possible. Knowing how many generations live together in a 'compound' is not enough. An understanding of the division of work and decision-making power of the various members of the household are also, and probably even more, important. Relationships between men and women often differ from those with which we are familiar, and the role of the elderly in the family is entirely different from the role elderly people play in Western society. And then there are their ideas and opinions about hospitality, which often conflict with our ideas and wishes regarding privacy and the hearth and home.

In a number of essays the subject of relationships with counterparts is mentioned. It is important to know the counterpart's job description and the nature of his formal relationship to the beginning expatriate. This is indispensable for the daily social intercourse. It may sound a little strange, but there have been numerous cases in which disputes occur because the expatriate's behaviour toward his counterpart was contradictory to the prestige the counterpart assumed to derive from his formal position. The opposite has also been known to occur.

Furthermore, you should by now realize that whites are often placed on a pedestal; this also happens in social life. Whites are honest, intelligent, rich. At least that's what the local people think. For many expatriates this causes many problems and they try to free themselves from this image as quickly as possible. It's not surprising that they don't often succeed; this idea is based on many decades of colonial domination, during which the African was constantly being told that whites are superior. This misconception has, regrettably, been maintained to the present day. My personal experience is that in the beginning there is not much to be gained from continually reprimanding the local people when they demonstrate too much enthusiasm for the white race. This missionary

146

work is best done through actions, not words. One must take care, however, as the danger of eventually living according to this idea of superiority may well become very attractive and real. Letting this happen is easier than you imagine. Most important is to be always on the alert and avoid abusing the fact that you will sometimes be revered. It is therefore advisable to acquire a certain knowledge and understanding of the social life of the group for which you will be working as soon as possible. The question now is, what can you do with this knowledge?

This brings us to the subject of the novice expatriates' 'ability' and 'being'. In several essays in this book, problems that result because development workers often think that they have to re-invent the wheel are discussed, and this is not without reason. They are often inclined to forget that a certain well-defined social structure already exists within a village or region, a social structure that has functioned for centuries and has, at least in part, enabled the people there to survive under the existing, often very hostile, conditions. Nothing could be more logical than using such a system as the departure point for development work. But this is not always done, to the detriment of the target group and the development worker himself. I would like to make one comment in this respect. The social structure of the group for which the expatriate is working is no less susceptible to change than are his own habits. It is possible that existing social relationships – one example is the relationship between men and women – are a stumbling block along the path toward a development supported by all parties involved. In that case the task of the development worker may be to bring the subject under discussion. There should be no misunderstanding about that. The point is choosing the right moment; it is of course still very important how the discussion is conducted. This book, however, deals with problems in the beginning period of the expatriate's work, and, in my opinion, there is no sense in a newcomer creating gaps in the fabric of the social structure of the society in which he works.

The responsibility of the beginning expatriate himself is also demonstrated by the following. Development workers are often trained on location by their predecessors, who have already formed ideas about the people concerned. They are like this or like that, you should or should not do this or that. One of the authors has justly pointed out that the beginning expatriate should be very careful about taking a stand. Of course he should be receptive to what his predecessor advocates, but at the same time he should not put aside his own ability to judge the situation. This all seems very logical, but if on arrival in that faraway country you feel like fish out of water, your first reaction may be to accept the well-intended advice of your predecessor as the gospel.

Last but not least, I would like to direct attention to another kind of problem, indicated by many of the authors, namely that of the social relations within the expatriate's own family. Every development worker who goes to a host country with his family should realize that each family member, especially the husband and wife, will have to depend strongly on each other in the new situation. A social life with friends, neighbours and family no longer exists. One finds oneself in a new situation where other expatriates may or may not be found. If

147

there are other expatriates, they often form cliques. Clique is used here to denote a group of people who work at the same project or school, but have not voluntarily chosen for this intimacy. Within these groups, peculiar social relationships often develop. They see each other often, whether they want to or not, and share a kind of compulsory brotherhood of fate, which in some, but certainly not all, cases develops into friendship. Fear of isolation drives one into friendships. The wives of expatriates in particular experience this problem. If the expatriate couple are the only foreigners in the region, a great strain is placed on their relationship, because they are entirely dependent on each other for the solution of their beginning problems. There's not much you can do to change this situation, but preparing yourself to face up to it may help. Of course, contacts with local people, not only on the job, but also in private life, are important to avoid isolation or undesired social dependence on other foreigners. Above all, it is prudent to state your justified wishes and preferences, as far as privacy and social relations are concerned, in no uncertain terms to other expatriates and local people from the beginning.

THE POWER OF MONEY: THE ECONOMIC ISSUE

Beginning problems with a cultural and social base have been discussed, but difficulties can also arise because of the expatriate's lack of knowledge of the economic characteristics of the society concerned. In this respect, I will give special attention to two subjects: first, to the economic structure of the society itself and, second, to the position of the expatriate within this economic structure.

Of the problems mentioned in this book, a large number can be put down to the expatriate's lack of insight into questions such as: who controls the economy in the village or region; who owns the shops; who owns the means of transportation; who owns the land; how is work divided; how is trade organized and what is the economic importance of the region for the national economy? I will try to illustrate some of this by means of an example. If you want to influence the local people in the Turkana region in the north of Kenya to become self-sufficient farmers, there are several things you must keep in mind. First of all you should know that the Turkana economy has, for centuries, been based on animal husbandry. Both Hans Visser and Gerrit Noordam acknowledged this fact, explicitly and in great detail. Furthermore, you should know that the Turkana, being herders, have no tradition of land ownership. Economic power has always been directly related to the number of head of cattle one owns. The Turkana have lost their cattle; this we are told in the essays. They are now extremely poor and bordering on starvation. This absolute poverty is the only reason that they are willing to try to cultivate crops. This decision is not based on a desire to become a good farmer, but on the desire to earn enough money from the proceeds of the crops to purchase cattle again as soon as possible. The economic structure cannot be changed within a day. The expatriate who is of the opinion that he can change it within two years will inevitably become very disillusioned.

Another example that may be of even greater interest to readers concerns mass migration from the rural areas to the cities in developing countries. We are often told it must be halted. This is not surprising as these mass migrations cause countless problems. But if one thinks that teaching 'agricultural science' at rural schools and asserting that life in the cities is miserable will check this migration, one will certainly be disappointed. As long as incomes from agriculture continue to decrease, due to, for example, lower prices and ownership of land by the few, the small farmer will be forced to look for alternative means of supporting his family. And often only one alternative exists: move to the city and look for a job there. The expatriate teacher at a farmers training college who thinks that he can change the situation by supplying a good education will without a doubt be disappointed.

But is knowing that the broader economic context is of such great importance of any use? Does this enable you, the development worker, to achieve better results? Regrettably the answer to this question will usually be no. One single person can do almost nothing about changing these conditions. But in the same breath, I must add that it is very important to be aware of the economic facts of life. It may prevent you throwing dust in the eyes of the people for and with whom you are working. You can point out that their alternatives are limited because the individual's economic behaviour takes place within a broader economic structure.

Naturally, the question of whether the economic structure itself should change arises. Assigning organizations as a rule require that the expatriate does not become involved in the politics of the host country. Obviously because of the basic nature of development work, this rule cannot always be followed to the letter. When one's efforts are directed toward improving the conditions of life of a certain target group, one is, sooner or later, faced with questions that have everything to do with politics. In my opinion it would be senseless to force yourself to avoid these issues. Once again, however, it is not the task of the expatriate to answer all questions for the target group. They will have to find the answers themselves. I will return to this subject in the next section.

Another problem, mentioned by a number of authors, concerns the economic position of the expatriate in the society where he is working. Of course, he is an alien element in the society concerned. A white man, well-dressed and living in a proper house, a white man who drives a car and can buy anything and everything he wants. He is surely very rich and must be able to share the surplus of his riches. It is, once more, very important to find out how the local people think about and judge you. This is a cardinal point in determining the way you approach these people. I am not primarily referring to an incidental lending of money to certain persons, but to the question of identification; with whom do the local people identify you? If your way of living and standard of life lead the people to identify you with, for example, the larger landowner or the elders of the village who control everything, all your work may be to no avail. The people will listen because it's considered polite and because they have always been obliged to listen to the large landowner. But your words will fall on deaf ears. You will, therefore, sometimes have to make an explicit decision about your conduct on the social scene and your standard of living. I'm not implying that you have to live in a mudhut and eat corn porridge every day. 'Going native', socially and economically, is no solution to this problem. What I am saying is that you should make every attempt to find out what your economic position is in the society concerned and transform this knowledge into a certain way of living. Once more we see that 'life is a great bundle of little things'.

TALKING ABOUT TABOO: THE THEOLOGICAL AND POLITICAL ISSUES

In the preceding section I have already made some remarks concerning the political aspects of development work. In this section, I will discuss these in more detail and, at the same time, include problems which have to do with religion and philosophy of life. The essays illustrate that a lack of familiarity with local religious experiences often gives rise to problems for beginning development workers. Some authors have repeatedly emphasized that it is not only useful but imperative to try to get to know as much as possible about the way people think about life, death and divinity, and to do this from the very beginning of your stay in a developing country. A knowledge of the deeper existential philosophy regarding people, animals and objects is important because in African cultures – more so than in the Western world – animals and objects have a certain meta-physical significance. One example is the importance that the Turkana attach to cows, another is that of seeds in the Pokot culture. A cow is more than just an animal and seeds are more than just objects, they are essential elements of human existence, carriers of a symbolic and metaphysical force.

Closely related to this we find taboo – the mystical, untouchable. Taboo is firmly rooted in the culture and the philosophy of life of some peoples and it would be most arrogant on the part of the development worker, who is after all accepted as a guest in the developing country for a number of years, to assume that he will be able to change this phenomenon within this short period of time. But the real question is whether he should even try. Once again, the problem of certain taboos that may form stumbling blocks on the path toward development may be encountered. However the question is whether a forced intervention in religious and philosophical systems, which have been accepted for centuries, would not sooner be destructive than constructive. This is a typical example of the kinds of problems touched upon in this book, problems for which no clear-cut answer exists. They must, however, be discussed, so that the beginning development worker is aware that he may well be confronted by these questions and will then have to choose his course of action. This choice depends strongly on the person involved and on the situation. No one other than the person involved has the right to decide.

The same is true of the position one takes with regard to 'black magic' and 'witchcraft'. Several years ago, I discussed this subject with a missionary in Surinam, whose opinion was that all of this is no more than 'primitive supersti-tion'. He prided himself on the fact that he was able to attract large numbers of

Indians to his little church to listen to gospel from the Bible. He seemed to have forgotten that the Indians liked an excursion once in a while, that they certainly enjoyed being fetched from their village by bus, that seeing the beautiful slides in the church was an experience for them and that the cookies he served in church after the service were definitely a great treat . . . He who makes light of other religious practices and behaviour by reducing them to the simplicity of superstition, thereby demonstrating that he has absolutely no comprehension of their social and cultural functions in the society, will probably never succeed in understanding that society. The result may be that the relationship that he is trying to establish with the local people is no more than a delusion, kept alive by both parties for a number of reasons, but one that can hardly be considered a firm fundament for a process of development. Moreover, when he returns to his own country, his presence there will remain in the memories of the people as no more than an insignificant incident in their unaltered lives.

Political complications are mentioned frequently in the essays. A distinction can be made between the political course chosen and followed by the receiving country and its influence on the expatriate's daily work. Western countries apply a certain policy when they engage in development co-operation. Some make very explicit choices, others exercise a much broader decision-making policy. Before you decide to go to work as a development worker for a certain donor organization, you will have to examine carefully the policy of the organization, for example regarding target groups and the countries with which the organization co-operates. In principle, you are under no obligation to apply for a vacancy or accept an offer if you have political objections to the nature of the project, the choice of country or the kind of education you will be expected to give. However the picture is not quite as simple as it seems on first sight. It is often very difficult to get the information you need to make a well-founded decision beforehand. You are idealistic, you want to work and you want to be sent out as soon as possible. That's the way things stand. You are bitterly disappointed when you discover that, in practice, things are slightly different. Beautiful and brotherly slogans often prove to be great disillusions when translated into guidelines for everyday life on a project or at a school. You may discover that you are not allowed to talk about politics at school, or that whenever a high-ranking government official visits the region all the schoolchildren have to show up enthusiastically waving flags. You may also find out that the project for which you are working is used as a prestige-object by the government of the host country when it suits them and is otherwise completely ignored and neglected.

What should you do? I can give no conclusive answer. My personal course of action would be to sit on the fence for a while, especially in the beginning. Interfering in these rather sensitive affairs too soon will often be counterproductive. Sometimes you will simply have to accept injustice for a long time, but this can be very frustrating. Nevertheless, the development worker should not continually violate his political conscience. A number of alternatives exist. He can try to discuss his apprehensions candidly with the people with whom he is in contact daily, but he can not decide for them. He can try to change the situation through the organization which sent him. And he can also resign, if he is convinced that he can no longer accept responsibility for the things he is doing. All these decisions have to do with the individual conscience and cannot be prescribed. The most I can do is suggest that a certain amount of reserve and a tactful attitude are important in the beginning. Also in these affairs, the conscience is and remains the inviolable refuge for human freedom.

LEARNING MANY LESSONS: THE EDUCATIONAL ISSUE

All of the authors of the essays in this book are rather intensively involved in the transfer of knowledge. Some give lessons daily, others are charged with the more practical kinds of training. It is therefore not surprising that many of the problems discussed in the papers have to do with education, in the broad sense of the word. Discussing all the difficulties in detail in this chapter would be impossible. I have therefore chosen to deal with a limited number of frequently mentioned problems and dwell on several in more detail. I will start with problems which have to do with the position of education as a social institution in society and thereafter deal with the course of events within the school.

Education, it seems, has a different place in African society than it does in the Western world. I will illustrate this by means of some examples. For many, education has the worthy reputation of being the way to escape from the poverty of rural life and acquire a well-paid job in the city. Much emphasis is therefore given to the element of competition and to obtaining a diploma. The desire to participate in education is often stimulated by external motives and not by intrinsic ones. In Africa, education is a means and not a goal in itself. There is much pressure on the educational system. It must live up to high expectations. This leads to much disappointment, as education is in general not formed and structured in such a way that it can actually fulfill these expectations. The pedestal on which the statue of education stands is made of cardboard.

Furthermore, education does not always respond to the learning needs of its recipients or of those who would like to be educated. It is often based on the colonial educational system, and there is much resistance to innovations in the nature of education, also on the part of the local teachers. Research into the real learning needs of the different groups of people involved in education would certainly lead to a better understanding, but is, on the other hand, considered a threat.

Another general problem, that has been rightly mentioned, is that certain kinds of transfer of knowledge clash with the existing culture in a village or region. In many cases, rural children have well-defined tasks in the daily struggle for survival. For example, they have to herd the cattle, or take care of younger brothers and sisters. Compulsory education disrupts this pattern and causes very practical problems. I have already mentioned that the system of education is often a faithful copy of the colonial educational system. This implies, for example, that children in former British colonies are required to wear school uniforms. Sometimes the parents cannot pay for the uniforms, or the children

152

have always worn skins, as in the case of the Turkana in Kenya. Education can then seriously upset the normal course of daily life.

What can you, the beginning expatriate, do in these circumstances? Probably very little. The national educational policy is an affair of the host country and in the past some countries have expressed their objections to expatriates who try to tell them what is wrong with their education system. Their argument is: we contracted you to teach physics or to teach the farmers how to plough with oxen and not to interfere in our educational policy. Those who cannot abide by this are better off staying at home. Here lies once again a task for the donor organization: to inform the departing development worker as realistically as possible about the state of affairs.

Although the beginning development worker may have little or no influence on the educational policy, he can certainly put his ideas about good and responsible education into practice at the school where he is working. More than that, I believe that it is his pedagogical duty to transfer knowledge in a way that is correct from a didactical point of view. This should of course be done in consensus with his local colleagues, in which case both parties will no doubt benefit. I will indicate several areas where such a dialogue can have good results.

First, attention should be given to the personal, as well as to the professional, relations between expatriates and local colleagues. Many complaints about the lack of motivation among local teachers, their reluctance to accept innovations in the existing system of education and their bias towards theoretical education and disregard of practical training are brought forward in the essays. It is understandable that the beginning development worker with his idealistic and progressive ideas regarding education may become frustrated. However there is another side to the story. Often the local teacher has been stationed at a school or training centre against his own wishes and far from his place of birth. In some cases, he doesn't even speak the same language as his students. His own training may leave much to be desired; often he himself has had a very theoretical kind of education and his apprehension at giving practical education can be largely explained by fear of the unknown. Finally, although he may not admit it, he may look up to the training and status of the expatriate. He has been told from the time he could walk that the educational system of the white people is the road to success.

As an expatriate you could of course reply 'that's none of my business; it's not my fault that things went wrong in the past; I have to work with this colleague now. I'm doing my best and expect him to do the same!' To me, this way of looking at the situation seems rather naïve and not at all useful in the real situation. Would it not be more sensible to accept the existing situation as a fact and to try and encourage a discussion with your local colleague to achieve at least some degree of understanding for each other's points of view? That should be the foundation for further co-operation. It is quite possible that the expatriate can then learn much from his local colleague and vice versa.

Any educational process of learning will benefit from a clearly stated formulation of learning goals for the short, intermediate and long term. These goals can only be formulated when and if there is some degree of clarity on the general

153

lines of the extent and content of the subject. It is possible that a part of the expatriate's task will be to develop educational materials, but a beginning expatriate will usually find himself in a situation where a certain tradition of education already exists. This is especially true when he is posted to a school or training centre. Whether his job is to develop new subject matter or to revise existing courses, the expatriate will have to consult often with his colleagues, who have been working in the field for some time. There is no sense in developing a course that you are capable of giving during your contract period, but that will be rejected by your local colleagues once you have left because they did not participate in its preparation and its contents do not comply with their wishes and opinions.

Naturally the same is true of the development and use of learning aids. Supposing you, as a teacher, had always used the overhead projector enthusiastically in your own country. You would like to introduce it at your school in Africa and are able to convince the director of the school to buy several projectors. You benefit and derive much pleasure from the use of the projectors, but forget to teach your colleagues how to use them, and about the advantages and disadvantages. What do you think will happen with this expensive equipment once you have left? I cannot emphasize enough that your stay in a developing country can only be meaningful if your presence there is more than just a temporary incident, but contributes toward the adoption of innovations that will survive and retain their utility, even after you have left.

I should like to conclude this section with a problem that is repeatedly found, namely that of the relationship between teacher and student/trainer and trainee. Beginning development workers are often distressed by the authoritarian approach that local teachers have towards their students. In the Western educational system more emphasis has in recent years been placed on democratic and liberal relations between teachers and students. Some beginning development workers think that these kinds of relationships can be applied in a developing country. This can cause problems. Misunderstandings arise between students and the expatriate because the students are used to a more authoritarian relationship. Misunderstandings may also arise between the expatriate and local teachers, because the latter feel that their authority is being undermined. Once when I discussed this problem with a priest, who has many years of experience with practical education in Kenya, he replied: 'The expatriates think they should be like a big brother for the boys they teach. But these boys don't need a big brother; they have enough of those at home. What they need is a leader, someone who will show them the way'. Although not everyone would agree entirely with this peremptory statement, it undoubtedly does contain a large amount of truth. Relationships of authority are well-defined in African societies and the teacher – although he may be younger than his pupils – is in a way considered a *mzee*, an elder, who deserves respect and has the right to command that respect. If the beginning development worker acts, especially in the beginning, as if he is someone who just happens to know a little more, but as far as the rest is concerned wants to be treated in the same way as his pupils, he will at the very least cause confusion. Is it not better, especially in the begin period, to conform as much as possible to the existing and accepted way of doing things. Of course you have every right to encourage changes but they will have very little effect in the long run if they are not also supported and practiced by your local colleagues. I suspect that, especially in this situation, the watchword of Gustave Le Bon is appropriate when he said that the only permanent revolutions are those of the mind.

AT THE OUTSET: THE PROJECT ORGANIZATIONAL ISSUE

Some of the authors who have contributed to this book were faced with the difficult task of starting a new project or part of a project. They present a large number of problems that can then be encountered. I will summarize their experiences here, this summary being limited to identifying problems that arise in the recipient country when starting a project. I am aware that many difficulties must be overcome in the planning phase, but going into details about these problems is regrettably beyond the scope of this chapter. Nevertheless, it would impossible to neglect them entirely, as problems of a project-organizational nature must sometimes be attributed to careless preparation and formulation of the project plan. To simplify matters, we will assume that the expatriate who is responsible for the initiation of the project has just recently arrived at his destination, his host country. From the essays, what can then happen to him? First I will mention several general problems that have to do with the fact that the project is a relatively important and new event in the lives of the people concerned. Thereafter I will discuss more specific begin problems – personnel problems and material problems, respectively.

He who thinks that all projects that can be considered development co-operation are enthusiastically welcomed by the people in the recipient country certainly sees only the bright side. Frequently and regrettably, projects are actually a new product that is imposed on the potential client by the Western 'traveling salesmen' in development co-operation. The Western world has enough money for development co-operation and people who want to work in developing countries, therefore a market must be found. Perhaps I am painting a rather negative picture, but everyone who is deeply concerned with development co-operation will have to admit that there is a great deal of truth in these comments.

That such projects are not always born out of authentic wishes on the side of the developing country in question does not mean that they are worthless. They may be of excellent quality, nevertheless the fact remains that the host country and the target group did not participate in the original planning. What are the consequences of this situation for the project? The essays demonstrate that one often has to deal with an obvious lack of motivation and distrust on the part of the people for whom the project is intended. Furthermore, the target group often has very high expectations. So high that the beginning development worker anxiously and fearfully wonders whether he can ever live up to them. This misguided pattern of expectations is understandable; it stems partly from tenuous rumours and feelings of hope.

What can be done in this situation? Naturally the target group should, in the first place, have been given the opportunity to participate in the planning of the project. But that is not always possible. Especially if the developing country forwarded the project proposal itself. Diplomatic considerations do not always permit the donor country to make radical demands of the government receiving aid, particularly if it is a bilateral project. A project can be formulated on paper in such a way that participation by the target group has been accounted for, but in practice the influence of the expatriate to involve the target group is sometimes limited. If the proposal is considered useful to both the donor and the host country and they decide to implement the project, the most the expatriate project staff can do is work within the general contours of the project plan. This, of course, does not rule out the possibility of actively and intensively seeking contact with the target group so that they too can participate in the implementation of the project from the beginning. In most cases this is absolutely essential for the success of the project.

This brings us automatically to the more specific begin problems in the organization of projects. In the first place, these concern personnel. It will be necessary to know a number of things beforehand: for example the laws dealing with engaging and dismissing personnel, what are reasonable conditions of work in a given situation, how is salary determined, which tribes have trouble co-operating with each other, what are the prevailing ideas about discipline on the job and absenteeism from work, are the job descriptions of the expatriate and counterpart clear, to what extent can and may responsibility be delegated? These are questions which can also be answered on location, but much time could be saved if the expatriate project director knew some of these things beforehand. It seems that there is still much room for improvement, also within the organization of the institutions that send people abroad.

Other specific problems are found in the form of physical attributes. Sometimes, even in the initial phase, internal contradictions exist between the goal and function of the project. This can result in the necessity of modifying the planned budget, which in turn may lead to much delay in the implementation. Difficulties can also arise in the administration of the project and the availability of the necessary donor funds. Problems with transportation and lodgings have already been discussed in this chapter.

Of course, we should realize that countless problems arise at the start of any new project and that this is quite normal and inherent to the initiation of a project. After reading the essays in this book and visiting a number of projects, I am absolutely convinced, however, that expatriates are sometimes sent into the field in a very careless fashion and then more or less left to their own devices, without efficient backstopping. It seems to me that the complexity of the situation in which the beginning development worker is placed is sometimes underestimated. I have often been amazed that young, recently graduated expatriates hold positions of great responsibility in developing countries, such as director of a school, head of a department, director of a project involving millions of dollars. In the Western world, at their age and with their limited experience, they would certainly never even be seriously considered for such positions. Managerial qualities that they do not yet possess are necessary. The demands made on their capabilities are even higher than those expected from a manager in a Western country. Management becomes especially difficult because it must be done in an unfamiliar environment where sometimes little co-operation can be expected. It is therefore of utmost importance that young, inexperienced development workers who will fulfill a management position are trained well and that they can rely on solidarity and sound backstopping from the home office. The question is whether the way in which this category of development workers is now being trained meets this need.

BEYOND WORDS

In the preceding paragraphs I have discussed a wide diversity of problems mentioned by the various authors. I have attempted to give a cross-section of the subjects they raised without lapsing into unnecessary repetition.

In the first paragraphs of this chapter I placed Plato's cave in the spotlight. Afterwards I have, in a manner of speaking, held mirrors before the eyes of the freed captives who stand blinking in the bright sunlight, mirrors which enable them to see one another. Moreover, they have also been offered a view of the landscape where the cave is located, and together they will explore this landscape.

I have also professed that I see little value in an extensive list of character traits and qualities to be required of development workers to assure that they will be able to function with at least some chance of succeeding. The danger then would be that one could easily start moralising. Moreover, every situation is, in its' own way, unique. On the other hand the fact stands that the experiences discussed in the various essays are of great value and, in my opinion, an attempt to regroup them and to abstract them from their context can be very useful, so that people who will soon depart for a developing country can learn from them. The recommendations and suggestions woven throughout the text are, of course, not based on fundamental empirical research. They are anchored in true-to-life experiences. Although not general and universally applicable, they do point in certain directions from which one can benefit in some situations.

The reader will realize, and I speak now on behalf of all the authors, that beyond our primary audience we have also addressed ourselves to those who take part in creating the conditions in which young beginning development workers must function. Nevertheless, we have no pretension of telling them exactly what to do. Organizations that send experts overseas generally have a vast reservoir of experience in this field and are constantly working to improve the conditions in which their expatriates must work. However some obstacles may be the result of certain traditions within these organizations or because of the limitations of the organization as an administrative unit. They can, however, function within certain boundaries and I sincerely hope that they too will benefit from this book.

A great number of experiences have been bundled in this book. In some chapters the authors have gone as far as to suggest guidelines for action. Now that I've almost reached the end of this chapter, one thing remains to be done. Or perhaps a word of warning would be more appropriate. The reader, who has studied this book carefully may now think, 'If I prepare myself for my work in a developing country in such a way that I can avoid the most dangerous pitfalls and snags mentioned in this book, I will have a good chance of succeeding and achieving my goal'. The teacher of a training course for development workers may well say after reading this book, 'If I succeed in treating the most important problems during the training course, then they will manage in the field'.

I strongly suspect that they have forgotten one of the most important conditions for the success of a development worker. This condition, however, is difficult to describe. It has to do with personality factors that are almost indescribable. Charles M. Schwab was perhaps very close to the truth when he said, 'Personality is to a man what perfume is to a flower'. This is also true of the relationship that the development worker must, by definition, create with the people for and with whom he is working. If he is not able to rise above a formal and functional pattern of interaction, he will much to his own surprise, not achieve that which he so strongly desired. This extra dimension which makes relationships satisfying and fruitful, also in the long run, is delicately illustrated in the following parable, which I read in an Ivorian magazine. It is a beautiful example of the richness of the African art of storytelling.

'There was once a young girl. Her name was Ama. She was very beautiful. She had decided that the man she was to marry must be very intelligent. Whenever a young man came to ask for her hand, she let him stay in a hut on the other side of the village. In the evening she would prepare a meal for him. And before she had it sent she would pick a leaf from a ficus plant, take a bamboo stick and a bone. She would place these objects on the lid of the pan with the food. If the young man had eaten the meal without understanding why he found a leaf, a bamboo stick, and a bone with his meal, she would send him away the next morning. And the young man would leave. Ama had done this very often. But there was also a young man, who in his own village, had made a resolution that the woman he was to marry should be very intelligent. One day he heard the people talking about Ama and he decided to visit her. He left his village, and when he arrived in Ama's village she sent him, as usual, to the hut on the other side of the village. In the evening she prepared the meal and sent it to him. She also sent the leaf from the ficus, the bamboo stick and the bone. When the meal was brought to him, the young man looked at the objects for a long time and said, 'The light of the moon and the dance have been united'. After he had eaten, he stood and picked up the three objects. He said, 'Now I will visit my wife'. He left and arrived at the entrance of a courtyard. A ficus was growing there. He said, 'This is the place' and tried to enter. Suddenly he was attacked by a dog. He threw the bone and the dog began to chew on it. He continued on his way. In the courtyard he looked around carefully and saw a small house with a door of woven bamboo. He opened

158

the door and went inside. The night passed and became day again. The girl said, 'This is the man I want to marry'. And the whole village began to make preparations for the wedding.'

14 ANNOTATED BIBLIOGRAPHY

Marco Hennis and Theo M. P. Oltheten

INTRODUCTION

A book like 'The Art of Beginning' might attract a very heterogeneous public. This was one of the conclusions of our discussions with the editor on preparing a reading list for this book. Some people might be quite familiar with publications on education in developing countries; they don't need suggestions for further reading. This chapter has been written for those who, just like the authors of the stories in this book, are starting work in development. To encourage further reading and to stimulate reflection, a selection of annotated publications can be useful.

Educational systems are man-made institutions. It is clear from the previous chapters that the process of improving educational facilities in developing countries is influenced by a wide variety of factors. The dedication, expertise and specific skills with which people in the field execute their jobs are very important, but that's not enough. The impact of their work is to a high degree dependent on specific characteristics of governments' policies for national and rural development. Although these issues have not been the main focus of this book, we agreed to include some publications on the more general background of national and rural development and the role of education, to present a more comprehensive picture of this very complex and broad field of study.

How do you go about making a selection out of the numerous publications, reports and relevant documents? We have approached this problem from a pragmatic point of view. A first group describes some publications on personal aspects of development co-operation, and on factors that play a part in the activities of development workers in the field. The selection of this literature is based on the findings of Marco Hennis' recently completed study 'The Human Factor in Development'. A second group describes a number of publications on agricultural and rural education in developing countries.

ANNOTATIONS ON EXPATRIATE PERSONNEL IN DEVELOPMENT COOPERATION

In the literature on development co-operation little attention is paid to the personal aspects of technical assistance. Major emphasis is put on development

160

projects and development strategies in general. However, since technical assistance programmes are becoming more or less institutionalized, the number of studies on personnel management, for example, personnel selection, and on cross-cultural adaptation have increased. A number of significant studies in this field are reviewed; most of these were written in the seventies.

Alexander, Y., 1966. International Technical Assistance Experts. A case study of the U.N. experience. Praeger Publishers, New York.

This work focuses on the United Nations activities under EPTA, the Expanded Programme of Technical Assistance. On the basis of information obtained in pre- and post-entry briefing sessions it examines the role of UN experts. According to the author this question must be seen against the background of a number of factors, viz. the size of the project, the applicant views, the UN's opinion on the appointment, the personality of the expert, professional attitude, the skills and attitudes of local officials and counterparts, adequate facilities and equipment.

Alexander adopts three broad categories of expert roles to permit a more meaningful analysis:
– experts whose primary objective is to achieve impersonal results
– experts endeavouring to achieve personal results (attitude change)
– experts responsible for achieving results in the administrative field.

The qualifications of the experts differ in nature, length of the assignments and in the level of the environment. The ideal expert is characterized by a combination of professional excellence and personal qualities such as a flexible mental attitude, openmindedness, patience, friendliness, modesty and communication skills.

Beemen, E. K. van & P. Barneveld, 1979. Motivation in Foreign Assignments. Institute of Cultural Anthropology and Non-Western Sociology. University of Leyden, 280 pp.

In 1976–1977 a study was carried out in the Netherlands on factors that influence the willingness of Dutch experts to accept an assignment in a developing country. The data was collected from a postal survey, in which 485 people ultimately took part. All respondents were registered as interested in a foreign assignment.

Results: The absence of continuity and career prospects in work as an expert is the first serious criticism noted. Work abroad is governed by temporary contracts. Another factor is uncertainty about the labour market upon the expert's return to his home country. It was also found that family circumstances (e.g. educational facilities for children) are frequently the cause of a lack of enthusiasm about accepting an assignment.

Byrnes, Francis C., 1965. Americans in Technical Assistance. A study of attitudes and response to their role abroad. Praeger Publishers, New York, 130 pp.

This study considers similarities and differences in the behavioural patterns of experts in cross-cultural roles in developing countries. It sets out to analyse relevant data on the relationship between the expert and his organization, his job/mission, the host culture and the local population. A long questionnaire, containing some 110 questions, was used to gather information for the study. The following list of chapter headings indicates the major areas of inquiry covered in this study: expectations and satisfaction; work performance; work-related interaction with nationals; work-related interactions with other Americans; learning in cross-cultural work roles; post-tour experiences and reactions of technical assistance specialists.

By analysing the contents of the respondents' replies, Byrnes breaks experts' attitudes down into various typologies:
- professionally oriented, usually those on their first assignment abroad
- oriented towards interpersonal and social approaches; most of the experts falling into this category have previous experience in development work
- oriented towards the administrative process of assistance
- oriented towards the job and the bureaucracy, and
- chiefly concerned with adventure.

Byrnes, Francis C., 1966. Role-shock. An occupational hazard of American technical assistance abroad. In: The annals of the American Academy of Political and Social Science, 368 (1966): 95–108.

Using his own study 'Americans in Technical Assistance' and six similar studies Byrnes describes a number of factors that have an effect on the phenomenon 'role-shock'. He reveals that experts working in developing countries often experience frustration and tension when performing their professional duties. Byrnes defines the phenomenon of 'role-shock' as the frustration and stresses associated with such discrepancies as between what a technical assistant views as the ideal role for himself and what he finds the actual role abroad to be. Major problems contributing to role-shocks are: ambiguity of the professional role; relating with counterparts; participation in the host bureaucracy; administrative problems with the assigning organization; and the complex demands of development.

Hawes, F. & D. J. Kealey, 1979. Canadians in development. An empirical study of adaptation and effectiveness in overseas assignment. Technical Report, Canadian International Development Agency, Quebec, 285 pp.

This research project covers three problem areas: the adaptability of Canadian development workers and their spouses; their receptiveness to the host culture; and the ability to transfer technology. The study has two specific objectives. First, to identify the components of effectiveness of work overseas, and second to develop a profile of expertise.

Environmental and organizational factors are not considered in the study, since it is primarily concerned with obtaining an insight into what individuals

162

can do to develop effective behaviour. Two sources of data were used. One was the opinions of the technical experts and their spouses and national counterparts on such general subjects as the transfer of skills, capacity for adaptation, selection criteria, expectations and preparation. The other source was categorical ratings, i.e. precoded questionnaires on experts, spouses and nationals.

Results: nationals perceived effectiveness of technical assistance as a function of intercultural – professional interaction, socially and on the job, and personal – family adjustment. Canadian experts perceived effectiveness as a function of professional competence, interaction with local culture and people, personal – family adjustment, social adaptation to compatriots – colleagues working on the same project and adaptation to the physical environment. The profile of the effective technical advisor is based on: professional qualifications, interpersonal skills, self assertion and realistic expectations before departure.

Hennis, M., 1981, 1982. The Human Factor in Development Vol. I – II. Ministry of Foreign Affairs DGIS/PD, The Hague, 220 p.

The first volume of this research project consists of a review of relevant literature on the functioning of development workers. A comparison of the findings of the various studies (those that are based on sound social-scientific methodologies) results in a set of categories. These categories represent a number of factors that determine the functioning of development workers:
– factors relating to the development worker himself (e.g. knowledge, motivation, expectations, adjustment)
– factors concerning the relationship between the development worker and his task
– factors concerning relations between the development worker and his colleagues, counterparts, team and local contractors
– factors concerning the social context in the developing country
– factors concerning the development worker's spouse and family
– factors concerning the assigning organization
– factors concerning the social context in the development worker's own country.

In Volume II a follow-up study to test the findings of Volume I emphasizes that – apart from personal and interpersonal factors – structural factors concerning the project, its location and the organizational level on which it operates all determine the activities of experts to a considerable extent. This study offers a systematic description of working and living conditions of development workers abroad. It is based on social research in which Dutch experts, either on leave in the Netherlands or in the field (Kenya and Bangladesh), served as subjects.

Iversen, R. W., 1979. Personnel for implementation, a contextual perspective. In: G. Honadle & R. Klaus (Eds): International Development Administration, Implementation Analysis for Development Projects. Praeger Publishers, New York.

The success of a project depends on the fulfilment of requirements in a wider environment in such a way that this environment supports the project and that continuity of the project is assured.

Successful staffing of a project partly depends on the extent to which the project attracts personnel of different types. Iversen attaches a considerable importance to talent and provides a number of guidelines on the identification and use of talent. These guidelines are:
– the best predictor of performance is previous performance
– it is important to establish a meaningful reward – motivation system to ensure the project retains its attractiveness
– project personnel are expected to learn, and they must have the aptitude for this
– allow future personnel to think about project design; participation often forms the basis of success
– the 'Gestalt' principle, i.e. the whole (project) is more than the sum of its component parts (experts). The members of a project team must realize this.
Some projects fail because of a lack of management qualities. With this in mind Iversen concludes by calling for a small-scale approach so that problems connected with mobility, recognition, motivation, the working discipline of experts and the inflexibility or complexity of project systems can be limited to some extent.

Ruben, B. & D. J. Kealey, 1979. Behavioural assessment of communication competency and the prediction of cross-cultural adaptation. International Journal of Intercultural Relations. 3 (1979): 15–47.

The importance of interpersonal and social behaviour for the successful accomplishment of a mission in a completely different cultural setting has long been stressed in literature. This empirical study sets out to provide scientific support for this view. It considers whether communication skills that are valid in Western countries have predictive value with respect to adaptation or success in another culture.

The concept of communication skills is operationalized in this preliminary study in terms of display of respect for another person; interaction posture; orientation to knowledge; empathy; interaction management; and tolerance of ambiguity.

The concept of cross-cultural adaptation is also defined. Three distinguishable views of adaptation are possible, viz. the dynamics of the culture-shock (referring to the extent, direction and magnitude of this shock), psychological adjustment (indicating a general feeling of well-being) and interactional effectiveness (the transfer of skills, participation and social adjustment). It can generally be said that each of the communication skills observed have predictive value with regard to at least one aspect of cross-cultural adaptation.

Schwarz, P. A., 1973. Selecting effective leaders of technical assistance teams. US AID, Washington, 40 pp.

164

The object of this study was to identify situations during a project that have a favourable or unfavourable effect on progress in the project as a result of the behaviour of the teamleader. In total 337 reports were collected. After an analysis of the contents of the interviews, eleven dimensions based on descriptions of specific behaviour were identified. These dimensions are technical qualifications (e.g. the ability to apply technical knowledge to practical and often very elementary problems); administrative ability (to keep on top of the situation in any circumstances); interpersonal relations (empathy and courtesy); motivation and drive (a personal responsibility for the attainment of the stated project objectives); acceptance of constraints, development commitment, character (e.g. personal integrity, honesty); personal security; stability; poise, backbone (in stressful situations defending your own position and conviction); and political finesse (the ability to hold the attention of colleagues, to be sensitive to undercurrents in the group).

Tucker, M. F., 1973. Improving cross-cultural training and measurement of cross-cultural learning. Volume I. Center for Research and Education, Denver, 130 pp.

This study elaborates, inter alia, on the concept of adjustment. According to the author this concept consists of affective, cognitive and behavioural elements. It is implicitly assumed that an adjusted development worker is also an effective one. Translated into emotional, intellectual and behavioural elements the following can be said of an adjusted technical assistant:
– informal interpersonal activities; the adoption of behaviour and habits from the local population and learning to appreciate such behaviour
– familiarity with local topics of conversation and being able to join in the discussion
– non-verbal communication: mastery of at least one local gesture
– having positive feelings about the developing country or the village in which he or she is working
– a positive attitude towards nationals.

ANNOTATIONS ON AGRICULTURAL AND RURAL EDUCATION

This group contains ten annotated publications on agricultural and rural education, covering a wide variety of interrelated issues. There is growing criticism of formal education as being inefficient and irrelevant to development needs. However, policy-makers in developing countries are confronted with several dilemmas that are very difficult to cope with if new, innovative educational strategies are formulated and implemented on a national scale. In most countries the preconditions for the effective implementation of these strategies are lacking. This situation is the result of many factors, in particular the very complex relationship between education and society, which is illustrated by analyses of the issue of education and agricultural growth and the question of agricultural educational facilities and trained manpower needs in the agricultural sector. A comprehensive and effective approach to issues like these depends on a detailed set of data from the grass-roots level, which is illustrated by a case-study of the school-leaver problem in Zambia.

To provide the reader with some information on different kinds and levels of agricultural education and training, two publications are included, one on residential farmer training in Africa and another on agricultural education and training at higher, intermediate and vocational level in different parts of the world.

Barwell, C., 1975. Farmer training in East-Central and Southern Africa. Training for agriculture; special supplement. FAO, Rome, 115 pp.

The purpose of this manual is to provide practical guidance to the teaching and extension staff of all agencies involved with rural development and the educational needs of the small farmer. It was prepared as a result of recommendations made by participants at national seminars and workshops in Ethiopia, Uganda, Kenya, Tanzania, Zambia, Malawi, Swaziland, Lesotho and Botswana. The central theme of these meetings was how to improve the functioning of residential farmer training centres, viewed from the experiences of the representatives of the different countries. In this manual the following subjects are discussed: different systems of residental farmer training centres; origins and aims of these centres; physical facilities; status of these centres and their relations with extension services; staffing and planning of training programmes; recruitment of farmers; relations between staff and farmers; courses of instruction; follow-up visits to the farmers; evaluation; demonstration; and finance. Basic data on all residential farmer training centres in the nine countries are included, as well as a short description of the main developments concerning these centres. A general bibliography and country reports and documents on agricultural education and training are included too.

Coombs, Ph. H., 1980. What it will take to help the rural poor. In: Ph. H. Coombs (Ed): Meeting the Basic Needs of the Rural Poor. The Integrated Community-Based Approach. Pergamon Press, New York, p. 1–41.

In his introductory chapter Coombs summarizes some of the major findings of an international research project, undertaken by the International Council for Educational Development (ICED) with the co-operation of officials in a variety of developing countries and external assistance agencies. From a comprehensive and critical analysis of nine projects in Bangladesh, Thailand, India, Sri Lanka, Indonesia and South Korea, an attempt has been made to shed some light on how to cope with implementation problems, e.g. how to convert good intentions into effective deeds. By the end of the 1970s the conventional piece-meal, top-down approach to delivering 'specialized' rural services had been replaced by a demand for a more 'integrated' and more 'community-based' approach to rural development, with the aim of meeting the basic needs of the rural poor. However, implementing this 'new consensus', as Coombs calls it, is an extremely difficult and complex task. The first important conclusion is that it is a must for anyone desiring to help the rural poor to get to know them, to appreciate not only their physical circumstances and needs, but also their social and political environment.

Another important requirement is to focus on the whole family instead of the individual. It also requires a realistic appreciation of the socio-economic and political structure, institutions, attitudes, and pattern of human relationships in each village, and an abundance of patience, persistence and courage. Second, the case studies demonstrate that different levels and types of integration are essential to the effective operation of any 'community-based' programme. Organizational decentralization and devolution of responsibilities are basic requirements for achieving better integration, especially at the lower echelons of the hierarchy. The case studies strongly support the point of view that extensive community involvement and self-help are indispensible for the success of projets and programmes. At the same time, however, it is clear that creating and organizing community involvement is very complicated because of the hierarchical social, political and economic structures of most villages. Different types and forms of community participation can be distinguished, as is illustrated by the case studies.

Third, a more integrated, community-based approach to rural development requires the recruitment, training and backstopping of a large number of front-line workers, such as village workers and para-professionals. The fourth point the case studies demonstrate is that the stereotype views of education have to be replaced by a more flexible, functional and integrated view of education, one that extends far beyond schooling or formal training courses, one that equates education with learning that may take many different forms. According to Coombs, voluntary organizations can effectively augment government efforts because of their relative independence and unique flexibility. Coombs concludes by making a number of recommendations and suggestions for development agencies if they are to pursue their announced rural-development goals effectively.

FAO/UNESCO/ILO, World conference on agricultural education and training. Volume I, Proceedings of the conference (201 pp.); Volume II, Regional papers (184 pp.). FAO, Rome.

The World Conference was primarily concerned with establishing a clear definition of the fundamental objectives of agricultural education and training within the context of rural and national development policies. The proceedings of this conference are presented in Volume I. During the conference three commissions discussed the following subjects: higher education in agriculture; intermediate agricultural education and training; and vocational training for farmers and related rural occupations. Reports of these commissions are enclosed in Chapter I. In Chapter II, addresses at opening and closing plenary sessions are presented, as well as commission papers and seven other plenary papers. Volume II is devoted to regional papers. They provide a broad survey of the main facilities in each region for all types of agricultural education and training. Special attention is paid to new ideas and trends that exist in the different regions and to the main problems that arise during implementation. The regional papers concern Africa, Asia and the Far East, Europe (both Eastern and Western), Latin America and the Caribbean, the Near East, North America, Oceania, the South Pacific Islands and the USSR.

Foster, Ph. & J. R. Sheffield (Eds.), 1973. Education and Rural Development. The World Year Book of Education. Evans Brothers Limited, London, 417 pp.

This final edition of the World Year Book of Education is concerned with rural development and education. Part I treats a number of general issues, some viewed from the perspective of distinct social sciences and some from a more diffuse practical experience. Part II deals with a number of case studies.

The articles in Part I cover a variety of broad issues, such as education for rural development (Wilson), emphasizing the vital role of agricultural education of the rural community, for women and girls in particular, in national and rural development. Anderson deals with effective types of education for agriculture, focusing upon the dynamics of agricultural processes and on what this implies in education for innovation and for diffusion of new practices. Schultz analyses different types of agriculture from an economic perspective and indicates the educational implications of each type. Hornik et al. focus their article on the role and use of mass media within different rural educational settings. From a systems perspective, Green presents an analytical framework to link non-formal learning activities with other activities that are an integral part of what he calls basic nation building. The issue of the role of schools and rural development is analyzed by Singleton from an anthropological point of view, supplemented by case studies of rural schools in Thailand and the Philippines. The topic of educational alternatives, of new ways for education in rural areas is the focus of Wood's article. Special attention is paid to out-of-school programmes for youth. Watts examines some general strategies to meet the educational needs of adults who are already committed to farm life. Evenson argues in his article on research, extension and schooling, that both formal and informal education will have only limited impact if climatic sub-regions are not prepared to invest in high quality and fundamental research. The last article of Part I contains an overview of a variety of recent developments in rural education, with quantitative data on agricultural education facilities at different levels in Asia, Africa and the Near East.

Transformational and radical models for rural development and the respective roles of education are exemplified in the case studies of Part II. China, Cuba and Tanzania have accorded education a central role in transforming their societies. The authors of the other case studies (Kenya, French-speaking tropical Africa, Madagascar, the Philippines, Burma, Malaysia, India and Japan) attach less importance to ideological questions and are more inclined to see issues in terms of economic incentives and market opportunities.

168

Gutelmann, M., 1981. Relations between education and technical progress in Agriculture: training of specialists. International Institute for Educational Planning, UNESCO, Paris, 83 pp.

The underlying objective of this study is to highlight some of the relationships between agricultural training of technicians and supervisors and technological progress in agriculture in Sudan.

The first part of the study is concerned with the general agricultural situation in Sudan. In the second part, attention is paid to the kinds of training required and the extent of the demand for supervisory and technical staff. The third part of the study is devoted to a description of the provisions of these specialists in agriculture by the system of education. Special attention is paid to the place of agricultural education within the general system of education, agricultural instruction at the senior secondary level, the higher institutes of agriculture and agricultural training at university level. The study is concluded by an analysis of the ratio between the supply and demand for agricultural specialists in quantitative terms, finding not only that the existing agricultural training establishments are incapable of supplying the required demand, but also that the current socio-economic situation in Sudan makes optimal use of these people very difficult.

Hoppers, Wim H. M. L., 1981. Education in a rural society. Primary pupils and school leavers in Mwinilunga, Zambia. CESO, The Hague, 186 pp.

This study explores some of the issues that are vital if a more comprehensive and effective approach to the school-leaver problem can be chosen. The first part deals with the recent history of the school-leaver problem in Zambia. The second part contains the body of research data about the pupils and school-leavers in Mwinilunga district. The third, and last, part summarizes the main findings and puts these within the context of local socio-economic development. It also compares the conclusions with those from similar studies elsewhere in Africa and suggests further hypotheses. The general conclusion is that the major influences, especially life-orientations, norms and values, appear to come from the home environment and that the school has only a minor – sometimes complementary, sometimes endorsing – impact.

The problem of the school-leavers appears to be not that they are alienated from the home community, migrate to town and become a threat to the social and economic order, but rather that they drift back to a stagnating rural society without being mobilized to help develop it. Therefore it is concluded that this problem will only really be solved once an overall transformation of the local society, and the society at large, is initiated, since that would not only make the whole education exercise more effective, but would also create opportunities for 'educated' work.

Malassis, L., 1976. The rural world. Education and development. Croom Helm, London/The UNESCO Press, Paris, 128 pp.

This study focuses on the relationship between development and education, the integration of the rural world into the process of development and of rural and agricultural education into the overall educational system. These themes are developed against the background of the 'transitional agricultural period' in many developing countries, which may be characterized by a high rate of population growth and a sharp increase of demand for food, while the methods used in agriculture are 'traditional'. From this point of view, the educational systems should play a crucial role in contributing to an increase in the productivity of agricultural labour. However, development requires more than education. Malassis advocates that the expansion of education must go hand in hand with the modernization of the socio-economic structures of agriculture. The desire for economic effectiveness, social justice and a more human society should make life-long education the corner stone of the educational system. The school should gradually be done away with as 'ruralized', life-long education for all is introduced. Unless society as a whole supports it, the chances of success are small. However, the real significance of educational reform is to be seen, writes Malassis, in the context of the dialectical relationship between education and society; once a society becomes aware of its evolving needs and decides to take action to supply them, the major obstacle in the way of educational reform has been overcome.

Simmons, J. (Ed), 1980. The education dilemma. Policy issues for developing countries in the 1980s. Pergamon Press, Oxford 1980, 262 pp.

This book reviews the evidence that is the basis for the growing criticism of formal education, and states the implications for policy-making in the 1980s. The two chapters of the first section of the book provide an overview of the central issues faced by planners and educators in most developing countries. Three categories of central issues are distinguished: inefficiency within the schools and the educational system (e.g. high dropout rates), mismatch between what the schools are producing and what the educational 'clients' need (e.g. unemployment of the educated) and inequities in the distribution of educational opportunities and results to the rural and urban poor. The education dilemma in developing countries is thus placed in an economic and political – rather than in merely an educational – context. The next three sections – twelve chapters, which comprise the bulk of the book – deal with such topics as efficiency of educational investment, the relation of employment, migration and fertility to education, and the problems of allocation, equity, and conflict in educational planning. The final section suggests a planning and consultation process to study and promote educational reforms. But, warns Simmons, one should not expect too much from educational research: 'There is no 'green revolution' in sight in education for most developing countries, because the 'product' is human, not vegetable, and can only be cultivated within a complex social, political and economic field. Putting more resources into educational research may help, but no educational 'high yielding variety' is expected to turn up, – let alone one that removes the political constraints on educational reform'.

Moulton, J. M., 1977. Animation rurale: education for rural development. Centre for International Education, University of Massachusetts, Amherst, 149 pp.

This is a study of *animation rurale*, an out-of-school adult education programme (agricultural education and training included), which has been implemented in most nations in French West Africa. The purpose of the study is to define the problems and issues of non-formal education programmes designed to enhance rural development in Senegal and Niger. The theory of animation rurale is described and some assumptions are identified and tested in accordance with the application in the two case studies. Based on conclusions about the effectiveness of animation rurale, six hypotheses are formulated about the pre-conditions necessary for implementing a comprehensive educational programme for rural development.

Wharton, C. R. Jr., 1965. Education and agricultural growth: the role of education in early-stage agriculture. In: C. Anderson & M. J. Bowman (Eds.), Education and Economic development. Aldine Publishing Company, Chicago, p. 202–228.

The fundamental question explored in this paper is whether certain kinds of education make the most appropriate contribution to agricultural growth in the early stages of economic development. The primary focus is on formal education, in particular the component of education that the author calls 'development education', the transmission of knowledge that is useful in the process of economic growth and development. A secondary focus is on the ultimate effect of development education upon farmers – the producers of agricultural commodities. Three kinds of developmental knowledge are needed by the farmers: knowledge about new inputs, knowledge about new techniques of production and knowledge about how to economize in production and marketing. Extension education should, according to Wharton, particularly concentrate on the third area because of the great need of farmers to implement the developmental knowledge provided. The difficulties of implementing the new knowledge of inputs and techniques is probably greatest in the economic realm because of the farmer's lack of previous experience in using the 'economic calculus'. These knowledge deficiencies of farmers regarding the economic tasks of farming are as great impediments to rapid agricultural and economic growth as cultural and institutional factors.

ABOUT THE AUTHORS

WOUT VAN DEN BOR (1949) studied agricultural sociology and education at the Agricultural University of Wageningen, the Netherlands. He holds a Ph.D. in Agricultural Science from the same university. He is the author of 'Island Adrift. The social organization of a small Caribbean Community: The case of St. Eustatius' and a number of publications on Caribbean sociology and rural education. His research interest is in rural education in developing countries.

JAN WILLEM BULTHUIS (1954) graduated from the School for Higher Agricultural Education in Dronten, the Netherlands. He taught a few years at the Kalulushi Farm College in Zambia. His main interests are plant breeding, soil science, land and water development and mechanization.

GOOF BUS (1932) studied sociology of the tropics and subtropics at the Agricultural University of Wageningen, the Netherlands. He worked on projects in Bolivia, Lesotho, Mauritius, Ivory Coast and Cameroon. He is a staff-member of the Royal Tropical Institute in Amsterdam. His main interest is in the sociological aspects of extension education.

THEO GROOT (1955) graduated from the School for Higher Agricultural Education in Dronten, the Netherlands. He works at a training centre of the Zairean Brethern Mission in Zaire. His main interest is in integrated community development and in anthropological research in rural village communities in Central Africa.

MARCO HENNIS (1955) studied social psychology at Leyden University, the Netherlands. From 1980 until 1982 he worked for the Dutch Ministry of Foreign Affairs on a study of selection criteria of technical assistance experts. Field work for this research project was carried out in Kenya and Bangladesh.

GERRIT J. KOESLAG (1943) graduated from the School for Higher Agricultural Education in Ede, the Netherlands. He has also studied agricultural economy at the post-graduate level. He worked a few years in industrial management. He taught several years at Barneveld College and was director of international studies at this college. His main interest is in the development of teaching methodologies for developing countries.

GERRIT NOORDAM (1952) graduated from the School for Higher Agricultural Education in Dronten, the Netherlands. Before he started working for the Dutch Reformed Mission in Kenya, he worked in agricultural extension education in Upper Volta as a Dutch volunteer.

THEO OLTHETEN (1953) studied development sociology at Leyden University, the Netherlands. He is the author of a number of publications on education, including 'Agricultural Education and Training in Dutch Development Cooperation'. His main research interest is in agricultural education and training in developing countries, with special emphasis on West Africa and Latin America.

PIET VAN DER POEL (1950) studied geography at the University of Amsterdam. He worked for FAO in Somalia and Botswana on soil and water conservation projects. He has published some articles on this subject and is currently studying for a Ph.D. at Columbus, USA. His main interest is in ecological problems related to landscaping and vegetation.

DAVID VAN DER SCHANS (1951) graduated from the School for Higher Agricultural Education in Dronten, the Netherlands. He also took a diploma course in land and water management. He taught several years at an agricultural training institute in Tanzania. At present he works as an agro-hydrologist at a Dutch research station for arable farming and horticulture.

HENNIE VAN DER SCHANS (1953) took a teacher training course for domestic science schools. She taught a few years in the Netherlands and filled vacancies in agricultural and secondary schools in Tanzania. Her main interest is in the basic subjects of horticultural training.

BEN VELDBOOM (1951) graduated from the School for Higher Agricultural Education in Dronten, the Netherlands. He taught a few years at the Chipembi Farm College in Zambia. His main interests are the biological aspects of small-scale farming and theology.

HANS VISSER (1944) studied history at the University of Utrecht, the Netherlands. He taught a few years at a secondary school in the Netherlands. He worked as a teacher for the United Church of Zambia and as a missionary for the Reformed Church of East Africa in Kenya. He did research on the culture and religion of the Pokot. His main interests are anthropology and African religions.

NICOLIEN WASSENAAR (1949) took diploma courses in childcare education and handicraft. She worked a few years in a medical children's home and in a hospital for children in the Netherlands. She participated in a community development project in West Cameroon before she started her work in the Northern part of that country.

WILLEM ZIJP (1948) graduated from the School for Higher Agricultural Education in Deventer, the Netherlands. He worked for two years as a Dutch volunteer in Upper Volta and thereafter in Lesotho for FAO. He holds a M.Sc. in agricultural extension education from the University of Reading, UK. His main interests are agricultural extension education and the development of visual aids.

174